Life After BROKENNESS

A Ministry Guide for Trauma Victims that Dissociate

DID - SRA - PTSD - Mind Control Programming

Life After BROKENNESS

A Ministry Guide for Trauma Victims that Dissociate

DID - SRA - PTSD - Mind Control Programming

MELODIE A. MOSS

 Davand Publishing

Copyright © 2017 Melodie A. Moss

All rights reserved. No part of this publication may be reproduced, distributed, or transmitted in any form or by any means, including photocopying, recording, or other electronic or mechanical methods, without the prior written permission of the publisher, except in the case of brief quotations embodied in critical reviews and certain other noncommercial uses permitted by copyright law. For permission requests, write to the publisher at the address below.

Davand Publishing

2600 Oakwood Dr. #264 Bedford, TX. 76021

More copies of this book and other titles by this author are available at Amazon.com and CreateSpace.com

Printed in the United States of America

ISBN:**069289022X**
ISBN-13: **978-0692890226 (Davand Publishing)**

*Cover images and design by Melodie A. Moss

DEDICATION

Life After Brokenness is dedicated to the One I'd move heaven and hell for to see whole, to all of the survivors of trauma that have shared their stories and trusted their deepest secrets with me and to the reader needing hope and answers. I wrote this with you in mind.

With All My Love,

Melodie

ACKNOWLEDGMENTS

First and foremost, I have to give praise and glory to God. Without Him, this book would not have been possible.

I must also thank the ones that have allowed me the privilege of their friendship and that have shared their survival stories with me. Without them, I wouldn't have the experiences I have had to produce the content in these pages. I honor your courage.

I would also like to thank my friends, "George and Pamela" that were kind enough to proof read and provide feedback and especially, George, an amazing man of God, who offered to write the foreword of this book. I appreciate your friendship and for the time you gave to this project more than you know.

Thank you to my wonderful friend, Olga, that has also done ministry with me numerous times. You are a treasure and I am blessed to know you.

To my friends, Pat, Rachel and Pam S., thank you for your encouragement and support.

Also, I would like to thank my family just for being them and for their understanding and support throughout the process of bringing this book to fruition. I love you all.

Table of Contents

FOREWORD i

INTRODUCTION 1

LET'S BREAK SOME STUFF! 5

ALTERS AND FRAGMENTS 9

THE IMPORTANCE OF BEING BELIEVED 21

KNOWING HEAVEN BACKS YOU 25

FOUR DIRECTION FORGIVENESS 33

DEALING WITH FEAR 43

DISCOVERING SELF WORTH 47

GOT VOICES? 53

CONCERNING DEMONS 57

DEVICES OF CONTROL 65

DISSOLVING SOUL TIES 69

ABOUT MEMORIES 75

RESTORING DECLARATIONS 81

MIND CONTROL PROGRAMMING 91

MORE SPECIFIC PRAYERS FOR YOUR CIRCUMSTANCES 95

FOREWORD

My name is "George." Today, I am a Christian minister and this is my story. It is a story of Life after Brokenness. Though I barely "believed" in God during my years of brokenness, one of my favorite Scriptures was a phrase in Isaiah 42:3 "a bruised reed He will not break and a smoldering wick He will not extinguish..." I couldn't believe God wanted to heal me, but I had enough faith to hang on to this. I knew God would not crush me or torment me as satan had. The verse in Isaiah goes on to say, "..in faithfulness He will bring forth justice." That is what this book is all about: God's desire to bring the justice of complete healing to the Broken. In the same way as the devil used human agents to devastate, God uses human agents to restore by the Power of His Great LOVE.

I began to "backslide" in 1979, but really ran away from God when my Father was killed in an accident the following year. I remember when I began to come back to the LORD, after 10 years of running away, it was like all hell broke loose against me. The process of God getting my attention was emotionally exhausting. On the rare occasion I couldn't avoid going to church, I would weep and weep during any kind of music. My dreams and thoughts were very troubled. I felt angry and depressed. I read every book on deliverance I could get my hands on. In the late 80's and early 90's this was a new subject in Evangelical experience. Nothing I did, fasting, prayer, isolation, tapes, books - none of it produced much more than momentary relief or none at all. Worse, some of it seemed to stir up awful demonic torment and oppression.

Ultimately, my wife began to try to find a medical answer, but I refused medication. After putting up with me for 15 years, she attempted to find her own relief in another relationship. Mine relief, however did not come for another 6 or 7 years. During that time I went from great instability, to getting a measure of my own deliverance and an emerging deliverance ministry, then back to a complete systemic disintegration. I became so buffeted by psychic pain that I literally consigned myself to demonic control by direct invitation. Whether through hallucination, in a vision or in a trance, I saw and felt horrific evil everywhere and ultimately lost my ability to resist any demonic attempt on my consciousness.

The most unusual part of these years of torment was that I would alternately feel, look and be able to act completely normal. Initially, the ritual component of my abuse experience was controlling. For me Halloween was one of the most terrifying days of the year. I believed that then, as always, I could be made to do absolutely anything – harming myself or even another person. I believed that my soul was like an open field and that any devil who wanted to could walk right over me.

Several in my extended family had experienced ritual abuse and 2 out of 3 of my siblings were sexually abused, though none like me. I witnessed others splitting into deeply fragmented personas, reverting briefly to infant or toddler behavior and communication skills. I had no sensation of losing time, but I knew that great chunks of my present-day life as well as my childhood were completely missing from my memory.

I will not describe the types of pains nor the hallucinations that accompanied them, but I sought many different ministers and ministries for relief and got none. One enduring and burning chest pain just would not go away. I became very familiar with many of the different methodologies in use for dealing with MPD, as DID was known at that time - both the secular and Christian methods. As a support person observing many different therapy sessions with Christian ministers I saw almost no relief for those receiving ministry and I saw ministers and counselors helpless to undo even the smallest part of cult, military or even trauma induced programming.

I one point I sought a secular counselor for myself, traveling from one side of the country literally to the other for sessions. I was so afraid of exposure. Months of effort produced little more than a deeper type of catatonic escape and recovery from the effects of these sessions was very time consuming. I became convinced that I could not possibly live long enough to go through all the process that many of these methodologies required. Through this all, when I was able, I cried out to the LORD for rescue.

Some time later, I went to stay for several weeks with a minister who worked with satanic ritual abuse victims and after that for a while, things began to become very manageable for me after that, but I still did not have the healing I now walk in. I did not even believe it was possible.

In 1996, I met someone that the LORD used to gradually impart a faith to believe for my healing. I was told, "It is inconsistent with God's character that He wouldn't want to heal you." I struggled with this statement for several years but finally I grew to accept its truth. By then I was determined to resist this "pulling" of my consciousness to the extent of my ability - I determined that I would "stay present" even though I constantly failed, lapsing into dissociative fugues.

The next year I became involved with a ministry experiencing full-blown Revival – meetings 6 nights a week, with thousands of salvations a week. My hope for healing began to rise.

Because of my history with the self-deception that surrounds dissociation, I decided to set the condition for my healing. I didn't want to experience something that looked like healing one day and then the next day feel that it had been stolen from me. I told the LORD that I needed to hear directly from Him that what I sought was actually happening – I need God to tell directly that I was healed.

10 months later, one Sunday morning it happened. The miraculous healing happened in a single moment. It came as the result of a visiting minister's extensive declaration of blessing from the pulpit. What was released on my consciousness at that moment was like the Tower of Babel in reverse. I went from many voices, and many languages to one. More than anything what I received was the gift of choice. Sure, I heard the Father say to me in an audible voice, "It is finished. You are healed." And on the heels of that astounding statement, I also heard these words, "But, it will be tested."

I finally experienced the miraculous healing (really deliverance) that changed my life. Soon, the physical manifestations began to cease, meaning I had control to deny them and I did that with regular success. I found I could choose to stay present, cast down vain imaginations, deny introjects into my consciousness. For several months, my healing was tested and challenged, but almost 20 years later, I am free and use the same kinds of prayers described in this book to help others like me get free.

Because of my own healing, I have faith for any kind of condition to be healed. I KNOW Jesus paid the price. I didn't need God to speak I to me directly, though He did; it's in His Word. Jesus said from the Cross, "It is FINISHED" and Peter, quoting Isaiah 53, confirmed it, "By His Wounds we were HEALED."

I'll never stop thanking Him for what He did for me.

My friend Melodie is relentless in passionate pursuit of God's purposes of the Abundant Life of Wholeness for the Broken. If I'd had someone like her, with her faith, my healing journey would have been vastly shortened.

I high recommend this work for its practical brevity and effective result. Jesus Christ sets the Captive free and He uses people like Melodie to do it. Really, God uses anyone willing to employ these tools by faith to uncover the treasure He's deposited in these Broken lives and usher them into Life After Brokenness.

DISCLAIMER

I am not a mental health professional of any kind, nor am I an expert in matters of the occult or mind control programming. My findings are through my interactions with those I've ministered to or through my own research. I can not guarantee that the suggestions within this book will produce the same results I, or others, have seen, nor am I responsible for any outcome resulting from following any advice within this book. I can not guarantee healing or restoration. As a matter of fact, apart from God, I can do nothing. He is the Healer. He restores my soul. Psalm 23:3.

*All scriptures used are from the New King James Bible unless otherwise noted.

INTRODUCTION

God is Love. Love is the most powerful force in the universe. It was love that caused God to send His only Son to save you and me. Love can cause you to do some crazy things. It can also cause you to find courage and strength you would not otherwise find on your own. Love makes us willing to make sacrifices and pay almost any price to help and comfort others. And for some, we'd move heaven and hell for love's sake.

I can tell you, it is not my years of ministry that qualifies me to write this book, but a burden to find answers to help just one soul that I love. My fervent prayers have brought answers and the Lord has moved a number of people in my path that needed answers too. Their willingness to share their stories and heartaches have given me a passion and a heart's cry to seek the answers, to bind up the broken and set the captives free.

This book is for those that suffer from Dissociative Identity Disorder [DID] brought on by trauma, Post Traumatic Stress Disorder [PTSD], Satanic Ritual Abuse

[SRA], or MKUltra programming or other forms of mind control and for those that would like to know how to minister to these victims. This book will not be clinical with a lot of psychological terms and theories, but a simple, practical guide with just enough information to understand and help those that dissociate. If you have no idea what this is about, consider yourself blessed, close the book and put this back on the shelf, but if you are aware of this form of mind's torment and want to learn how to help others or even yourself, I believe you'll find this book invaluable.

Ministry to people with dissociative identity disorder [DID] or multiple personality disorder [MPD] can be very delicate and complex. People don't just wake up one day with this problem. It comes about due to traumatic experiences that shatter the soul of a person. Sometimes, especially with SRA victims, demons are purposely invoked, adding another layer to the process. I believe if the Lord, Himself, stood before these victims, He could free them completely with just a few simple words or a touch. I find it incredibly frustrating that I have yet to minister as easily as I believe the Lord could, but I do believe that is available for us in Christ and we should be able to minister effectively and efficiently and see immediate results every time. That's the ideal. That's what I strive for, but I haven't arrived to that place yet. With some, I have seen amazing progress. With the most traumatized and demonized, it can take a lot of time and be a huge commitment. Because I am only one person and the need for this type of ministry is greater than you can imagine, I am sharing what I know and the revelation the Lord has given me to help equip you to minister to this need as well. I believe that this book may be able to help people minister effectively to themselves and perhaps this type of ministry can even be done in group settings.

I suppose this sort of work can be done by simply applying the information in these pages. Jesus' disciples were able to heal and cast out demons without being spirit filled, however, I strongly suggest if you aren't a Christian, you repent, receive forgiveness of your sins and accept Jesus as your Lord and Savior and ask for the indwelling of the Holy Spirit. He will be your best friend and guide you as to how to pray and minister. You can learn your part, but it is He that saves, delivers, heals and frees captives. You're going to need Him whether you minister or not. He is vital to life. Just speak to God from your heart and if you don't know how to start, here is a sample prayer...

God, I have come to a place of knowing I need You in my life. I ask You to forgive me of my sins against You and others. (It might be beneficial for you to speak these out to clear your conscience.) I receive Your forgiveness. I believe Jesus died for me. I believe He took stripes upon His back for my healing. I believe He died in my place, took my punishment, and rose from the dead. I ask that You come live inside of me and fill me with Your Spirit. Thank You for Your forgiveness and receiving me as Your own and for staying with me all the days of my life. Amen.

Just as a spirit filled person begins to speak and expects Holy Spirit to fill his mouth with words, I believe, even as I share my many notes with you, that the Lord will move my pen, if you will, to bring more revelation as I step out in faith and we share this journey together. May we bring His light to their darkness and His healing to their hearts.

Ready? Let's break some stuff!

LET'S BREAK SOME STUFF!

I'll explain in a bit, but the first thing the Lord ever showed me directly in this type of ministry is to break the triggers. Now each time I begin with a person I've never ministered to before for dissociation, I give some commands. I suggest that you make this a practice as well. If you are ministering to someone else or to yourself, just give some simple commands like the following and if you're not familiar enough with their background and what type of trauma they have been subjected to, I'd suggest you speak it all out.

It is important that the person be present or can hear the commands audibly and you must give these commands with the expectation when you say them, that the triggers will be broken. If you are saying these over yourself, just change the wording a bit so these commands are directed to you personally.

BREAKING THE TRIGGERS COMMANDS

I bind and break every trigger, every trigger word, every image, every cue and hypnotic suggestion RIGHT NOW! I bind the power of mind control and I command it to be broken and of no effect. Any manipulation or witchcraft, I bind and break and render it null and void! It has no more power over you. Any devices that have been implanted in you to control you, whether they be chips, pins, webs or ports, I break their power over you. I bind any demonic activity in and around you. I bind any effects from alcohol or drugs and command them to be broken. I bind any programming that you've been subjected to NOW! I declare your mind is free from binding influences and you are now able to think clearly for yourself.

So what was that all about?

Just as a song on the radio can bring back a memory of another place and time or the smell of certain foods can remind you of home, our senses have a way of triggering memories in our mind, both good and bad. Because some form of trauma is the source of dissociation, causing the soul to literally fracture, triggers can be hell for the victim causing them to either relive the trauma and/or alter to cope as that memory surfaces. Triggers can be anything that reminds one of a traumatic event. For example, fireworks could trigger a combat vet. A dark stairway or a certain cologne could trigger a rape victim. A dead animal, blood, a cross, candles, even the name of Jesus and any number of other things could trigger a SRA victim. And there can be a number of words, cues or images that might trigger someone subjected to mind control. Anything a person can perceive with their senses could bring back to their memory details that can overwhelm them at any time. These triggers can shut down a person and close them off from receiving ministry. I understand why the Lord spoke to me about breaking the triggers first, as it allows an individual to more readily receive ministry and help. Also note that the commands listed above have no mention of Jesus in them because it is very common in programming and in SRA to repel anything involved with that name, therefore I break the triggers without saying, "In the name of Jesus" so that the mind can receive the commands without blocking them. After they are broken, use it all you want.

As we get more detailed in the book about specific ministry for various trauma conditions, you'll see why a blanket faith command to break any trigger is helpful as no two stories or circumstances are alike. If you could disarm the weapons of an attacking enemy, wouldn't you? This is an effective means to help with that, so I will refer back to this again.

A word of caution: As you engage in this process, you or the one receiving ministry may find themselves being triggered. Just as a dentist may initially cause one to be uncomfortable in the process of repairing a broken tooth, the result will be worth the discomfort. You are in a safe environment. You are taking control of your life. You have decided to do what is necessary to become whole. Whatever happened to you was not your fault. Be kind and understanding to yourself. If you feel like you are triggering, remind yourself that this will pass and that you are safe. You may want to wrap up in a blanket, slow your breathing, focus on an item, perhaps a piece of jewelry that you didn't have during the time of the trauma and keep your mind on the present. Listen to calming music or step away for a bit if needed. Prepare yourself to come back to read this section again and if you're trying to do this on your own, now might be a good time to get someone you trust and a believer in Christ to help you with this. Be patient and determine to go through each step deliberately. The wall will eventually fall.

ALTERS AND FRAGMENTS

By definition Dissociative Identity Disorder (DID) previously know as Multiple Personality Disorder (MPD), is a mental disorder in which there are a minimum of two distinct and relatively enduring identities or personality states that show in a person's behavior. Some also refer to it as having a split personality.

The disorder is most often a result of extreme and repeated trauma sustained by a child during their more formative years, between birth and the age of eight. It could be inflicted by the loss of a parent, any or all forms of abuse including sexual abuse, and in some cases satanic ritual abuse or mind control. It is possible for an adolescent or an adult to sustain trauma and dissociate as well. Statistically, females are far more likely to experience sexual abuse, therefore they are up to nine times more likely be diagnosed with DID.

An interesting fact is that DID is likely the least studied and most debated psychiatric disorder out there. Although most psychologists seem to feel that DID is a valid diagnosis, over a third feel that DID could be created through a therapist's influence and up to 15% feel that DID could likely or definitely develop as a result of exposure to various forms of media. Some mental health professionals feel that some victims actually suffer from False Memory Syndrome (FMS), a condition in which a person's identity and relationships are affected by memories that are factually incorrect, but that they strongly believe. So the debate rages on.

Depending on the source you read, it is generally believed that anywhere from 1-3% of the population is affected by DID. It isn't as rare as many believe. As more stories of childhood abuse surface, the percentages may go as high as 10%.

Symptoms of DID can include, chunks of memory loss, depression and self harm, including cutting and suicide attempts. Victims may also be alienated, try to self medicate and struggle with substance abuse or may have an inability to function in school, work or relationships. Approximately one third affected may experience hearing voices and auditory or visual hallucinations, including that of a demonic nature. They may be prone to nightmares, loss of appetite and oftentimes they push people away, including those that love them.

Imagine a glass, perhaps a stemmed wine glass, somewhat fragile in nature. Let's say that this wine glass represents the human psyche, the soul or mind of a person, their true being, inner person, the center of thought, feeling and motivation. From this point forward, we'll refer to this as the CORE person, who they really are.

Now this glass, this core person, sustains a trauma. As an

example, let's use an instance where a young child is being sexually assaulted. The child may be experiencing pain, confusion, have no idea what or why this is happening to them. He or she may wonder why they are being punished, what they did and why this person they trusted is doing this to them. This event may be so overwhelming to them that their core person, to protect itself, goes inward and hides. Perhaps, as a self defense mechanism, another personality factor rises to the surface, like rage or anger, to deal with the perpetrator. Some sort of event causes damage to the core and something breaks and shatters the glass leaving broken pieces. If the broken piece is large enough that a personality develops from said trauma, it is referred to as an alternate personality or an alter for short.

An alter may have various differing characteristics than that of the core person. Alters may seem like an entirely unique personality with their own distinguishing traits. These may include different names, preferences, ages, accents, mannerisms or talents. They may also be of the opposite sex than the physical body. They may have different roles and functions and hold different memories than other alters or the core person. Victims often have a number of alters depending on the severity of the abuse.

When a glass breaks, there are oftentimes very small pieces left in the wake. With DID there are often fragments of the soul as well. Not a defining piece like an alter, but a piece just the same. To simplify this as much as possible, we will use the terms core, alters and fragments throughout this book. I invite you to research to your heart's content, but I believe Jesus would keep it simple and not overcomplicate this. It is complicated enough already.

There are other terms used in the mental health world, but for the purposes of ministry, We are not calling on the world for their help, but upon the Kingdom of God.

Let's look at **Isaiah 61:1-3 "The Spirit of the Lord God *is* upon Me, Because the Lord has anointed Me to preach good tidings to the poor; He has sent Me to heal the brokenhearted, to proclaim liberty to the captives, and the opening of the prison to *those who are* bound; to proclaim the acceptable year of the Lord, and the day of vengeance of our God; to comfort all who mourn, to console those who mourn in Zion, to give them beauty for ashes, the oil of joy for mourning, the garment of praise for the spirit of heaviness; that they may be called trees of righteousness, The planting of the Lord, that He may be glorified."**

The victims of trauma certainly are brokenhearted, captive and bound. The Lord came to set them free. Now, we are His representatives. As He is so are we in this world. The full verse in **1 John 4:17** reads, **Love has been perfected among us in this: that we may have boldness in the day of judgment; because as He is, so are we in this world.** Love is the key. Compassion is what makes us want to see this person healed, whole and completely free regardless of how complicated it appears. It is Holy Spirit in us that guides us and our job is to follow His lead. He wants that person set free more than we do.

Placed in the trust of God, someone so broken can be bound together like the pieces of a puzzle. He remembers the image and still sees His design within a broken soul. Piece by piece a person can be fearfully and wonderfully made again, even stronger than their former self. In the **23rd Psalm**, there is a passage that resonates. **He restores my soul**. No matter how hurt or shattered you are, He made you and He can fix you. Take heart in that. This book can help you get there.

Alters can be formed a few different ways. One way is by being harmed by direct abuse or trauma such as being beaten, tortured, sexually abused or raped. They can be formed when the mind is overwhelmed during acts of war, due to severe shock at the loss of a loved one, or seeing some event or carnage your mind can't process. Alters can be birthed from being used or participating in a satanic ritual, by being a crime victim or by methods of mind control. The person's core can't sustain the pain of the trauma and so an alternate identity is created from within to bear what the core can not withstand. Alters created by an abuser or programmer can also be set in place to protect a cult secret.

Another way an alter can be formed is when someone is forced to do or take part in something they don't agree with and are strongly against. A couple examples of that are when a woman is raped and intentionally impregnated to be a "breeder" during a satanic ritual. A breeder is used to carry a baby to full term. The due date is often targeted to coincide with a particular day on a satanic holiday calendar like Halloween or summer solstice. The newborn is used as a sacrifice to satan and sometimes the mother is forced to kill her own child(ren). Another example is when a young boy is sodomized by his own father and then prostituted out to other men to do the same and being forced to do a number of horrendous acts for large sums of money.

Other ways alters can be formed is by intentional

programming. Some names for this are MKUltra, MKSEARCH, ARTICHOKE and Project Bluebird. These methods have been used by the CIA, the military and even in the entertainment industry. Some research experiments include torture, insertion of brain electrodes to control subjects, forced drugging, hypnosis and training one to behave as commanded by trigger words, cues, images as well as a number of other ways. MK-Ultra is an Illuminati program used to intentionally inflict trauma to brainwash children and adults so they can serve as terrorists, assassins, sex slaves, sex blackmailers and entertainers.

What?! Why would entertainers, singers and movie stars be on this list? Lets look in **Ephesians 2**, starting at verse 1...

1 And you *He made alive*, who were dead in trespasses and sins, 2 in which you once walked according to the course of this world, according to <u>the prince of the power of the air</u>, the spirit who now works in the sons of disobedience, 3 among whom also we all once conducted ourselves in the lusts of our flesh, fulfilling the desires of the flesh and of the mind, and were by nature children of wrath, just as the others.

Here we see satan referred to as "the prince and power of the air". So what does that have to do with this? What is in the air to be prince over? Air waves! Television and radio signals, WIFI and phone signals are influences that we are bombarded with every day. Remember back in the day when people talked about subliminal advertising? They used examples of movie theaters showing hot desert images on the screen and then flashing a cold soft drink image on one frame and people would fly to the concession stands before the movie started. That is just the tip of the iceberg. Imagine the enemy controlling all of the music, commercials and film you hear or see by literally programming the individuals behind the cameras and microphones. It seemed far fetched to me too until I met and ministered to some victims of this. It really does happen. There is an agenda. They really do take the starry eyed kid that says, "I'll do anything to be famous." Anything? Well, some of the ones that tripped into this are trapped and want to get out now. The price of fame is very costly. I dare say in most cases, if someone in the entertainment industry is a household name, they are put there and controlled by the powers that be, working for the prince and power of the air.

Celebrities are very influential, especially to younger fans. People want to dress, look, act and perform like them and lots of money changes hands because of it. They aren't referred to as idols without reason.

If you know what to look for, you can see celebrities alter in interviews and performances. They may speak with different accents or seem to change behavior in mid sentence. Sometimes programming fails and we see many celebs, mostly in their twenties or so, falling apart at the seams. Usually when this happens, you'll hear of an entertainer being sent to "rehab" where they are reprogrammed and turn up later, a bit less messed up than before they went. Some celebrities rebel and want to get out of the industry. To control them, their reputations are run through the mud in the media and oftentimes their families are threatened. For the famous, it takes a lot to leave that control and few get out alive. Not all suicides and drug overdoses are what they seem. In very rare cases, some have faked their own deaths to escape. Those that try to climb out of the system often get sucked back in because the pressure and risk is so great. Research this for yourself. You'll see there is quite a can of worms to explore. Most importantly, as a minister, you need to understand this sort of thing really does happen. We have to understand what exists, before we can learn how to help.

So if the traumatic event is over, why do alters stay?

There are a few reasons why alters remain after the traumatic incident is over. One is to protect the core from a possible perceived reoccurrence. Many victims of abuse are subjected to repeated attacks in which the alter takes the brunt of the impact to protect the core. The alter is there to stand ready against a possible threat, even years later.

Another reason an alter might stay is because they know they hold a piece of the puzzle only they possess. Going back to the broken glass analogy, it is impossible to put a shattered glass back together without all of its parts. The alter knows they hold a needed part of the mystery of the victim's psyche for them to be made whole. They long to have the opportunity to help and share their part of the puzzle and reveal the secrets they have when the mind is able and strong enough to receive it.

Sometimes an alter is created and set in place purposefully to protect cult secrets. Young minds are trained with betrayal programming, not to trust anyone and even to betray others. Their savior figure, one they are taught to trust, will also betray them. The method they use is heartbreaking. Programming is a very intricate process with multiple levels of hidden structures, symbols, codes, booby traps, idols, guards, rooms and doors formed in the mind to prevent freedom. Thankfully, with God ALL things are possible to him that believes!

Another reason that an alter stays is because it cries out for justice. Let's look at some scripture...

Genesis 4:8-10 Now Cain talked with Abel his brother; and it came to pass, when they were in the field, that Cain rose up against Abel his brother and killed him. 9 Then the Lord said to Cain, "Where *is* Abel your brother?" He said, "I do not know. *Am* I my brother's keeper?" 10 And He said, "What have you done? The voice of your brother's blood cries out to Me from the ground. 11 So now you *are* cursed from the earth, which has opened its mouth to receive your brother's blood from your hand.

Here we see that the voice of Abel's blood cried out to God from the ground. There was no longer any life in his body, yet the blood cried out to God for justice.

Revelation 6:9-10 9 When He opened the fifth seal, I saw under the altar the souls of those who had been slain for the word of God and for the testimony which they held. 10 And they cried with a loud voice, saying, "How long, O Lord, holy and true, until You judge and avenge our blood on those who dwell on the earth?"

Again, we clearly see cries for justice in this passage. From the beginning, man has something innate in him that understands right from wrong. When he is wronged, he can cry out to God, knowing it is He that can bring justice and right the situation. In **Luke 18**, we find from the parable of the persistent widow this assurance from Jesus,

6 Then the Lord said, "Hear what the unjust judge said. 7 And shall God not avenge His own elect who cry out day and night to Him, though He bears long with them? 8 I tell you that He will avenge them speedily.

An alter may know that an injustice was done and cries out for justice. Until that is healed and mended by God, the brokenness will remain. The Lord showed me that this is an integral key to wholeness. It is only God that can give justice and peace to the heart of man. It is not our job or place to right a wrong, but to direct it all to the Lord. Lets look at this from **Romans 12:17-21...**

17 Repay no one evil for evil. Have regard for good things in the sight of all men. 18 If it is possible, as much as depends on you, live peaceably with all men. 19 Beloved, do not avenge yourselves, but *rather* give place to wrath; for it is written, "Vengeance *is* Mine, I will repay," says the Lord. 20 Therefore "If your enemy is hungry, feed him; If he is thirsty, give him a drink; For in so doing you will heap coals of fire on his head." 21 Do not be overcome by evil, but overcome evil with good.

Some alters will stand guard to protect until the threat has surely passed. An alter may wait to share and disclose what it knows when it is safe to do so. Some are trapped in programming and some alters cry out for justice and healing on behalf of the core and the sum of all of its parts. It is then that they can be put to rest and integrate with the core person.

A few more tips on communicating with alters...

When it comes to an alter's age, it is my experience that if an alter gives you an age, especially if it is the age of a young child, that is oftentimes the age the person was when the trauma occurred creating that particular alter. Therefore, the younger the age of the alter, the longer it has been with the person, actually making it an older alter. Very young alters often talk like a child or even baby talk. I have known both men and women to do this.

Just as different people have different tolerances to pain, some have different tolerances to traumatic events. For example, a harsh word, a slap or watching a pet die may be very traumatic for one person and may cause dissociation, where as someone else may have a much higher threshold before they were to alter. Regardless of the person's story or history, whatever caused their trauma is very real and hurtful to them. In the highly dissociative, for example, some alters can create a brand new personality just to answer a phone they don't want to answer. It is not our place to judge or belittle, but to help and minister God's love to them.

Alters can give you parts and pieces to a puzzle that neither the core person nor other alters or fragments can give you, so it helps to take notes when ministering and it is advisable not to disregard what you learn from each facet of the person before you. Alters often refer to the core as "he or she, him or her". They often refer to other alters or fragments as "others" and sometimes refer to the group as "we", although they are aware others exist, they know very little about them or their experiences. It's as though they are compartmentalized. Some alters are fearful of others, as sometimes there is one that bullies the others. The bullies are usually ones that are demonized, but that's another section. The alters are almost always very protective of the core person, as that has been their purpose from the beginning. They have also been known to tattle on the core and report things that either the core is afraid to disclose or ways in which the core is being self destructive. For instance, one alter very flippantly reported to me, "She is pregnant and afraid to tell you." Other alters have reported cutting instances, overdoses or suicide attempts. Remember, their job is to protect the core in spite of themselves and new trauma, even self imposed, can cause the core to create another alter or at least have no memory of the incident. They may come to their senses not knowing what happened. Loss of memory is a coping skill, but some victims lose large blocks of time; a tragedy in itself. Imagine living all your years and only remembering half of it and being unable to figure out what's missing. Imagine waking up to chaos, seeing evidence you even caused it, but having no idea what happened; a nightmare you wake up to, not from.

I am reminded of that old nursery rhyme, "Humpty Dumpty sat on a wall. Humpty Dumpty had a great fall. All the king's horses and all the king's men couldn't put Humpty together again." It may seem that no one can put you back together, but I assure you, THE KING can! He created you and He can restore you and He can do it through His children. Take heart, if you have Him, you know the ANSWER!

THE IMPORTANCE OF BEING BELIEVED

Little Secrets

Of course I knew him.
Then one day I learned about the sordid secrets
    adult men can have with little girls.
What did he want with me?
I had a thin rectangular body with limbs, flat on both sides.
At eleven, I had not yet considered how to please a man,
but he showed me where he wanted to be touched.
So scared and sick–
when I recoiled, he thrust my hand there again.
When his hand was not over my mouth,
his stubbled chin scraped against my face as he forced kisses
while his hand slipped under my blouse and moved
to where my chest might have been if I were older.
His breathing was heavy, rapid and so hot.
I could not breathe, but could smell his putrid cologne.
I can still smell it.

The adult I am now would have fought back,
but the child there was frozen
until a knock on the door allowed escape.

I later told my mother.
She punished me for telling stories like that about such a nice man.
I had never told stories before.
I never told her anything again.
I could have kept telling until someone believed me,
but the damage was already done.

The above is a poem I, myself, wrote a number of years ago about an experience from many years before that. One incident of many from more than one man and yet, my stories are very tame compared to the numerous ones shared with me during ministry. I and many others, male and female, have been someone's dirty little secret far too many times. It adds insult to injury when no one believes you. Sometimes abuse is coupled with threats, not just toward you, but against family or loved ones.

"You shut up and never tell or I'll do this to your sister."

"You will do it or I'll kill your mother."

"You say anything at school and I'll pack your ass up and send you somewhere no one will ever find you."

"Look at you! Do you think anyone cares? No one will believe you anyway."

Sentiments like this, along with hidden bruises or scars can keep a child in fear and compliant. If you exert enough force and threat, it can work with adults too, I assure you.

When it comes to a child that is somewhat dependent on others for the basic needs of life; food, shelter, clothing, schooling, healthcare, etc., and they don't have the physical strength to defend themselves nor the ability to take care of their own financial and other needs, they are at the mercy of adults to see to their survival. The problem and the number of children in crisis is so great, agencies turn away kids back to the offending parties all of the time because there is no place for them to go. When they are in an abusive household or situation, then it is the ones outside of the home that become a hope for their well being. If other relatives, neighbors, the schools or agencies can't or won't step in to rescue the child, then these fears and horrors can fester and exacerbate the problem for years until the grown child is able to break free on their own and left to deal with the emotional aftermath the best they can.

One of the most important things we can do for someone is to listen, to believe them and to understand their story may seem too horrific to be true, but it is and they need to be heard and accepted. Also know their stories may have holes in them, but that is because a fragmented soul doesn't have all of the pieces and parts of their truth themselves. Love them through it and be patient. They desperately need that. They expect you to say all of the things they've heard before like, "You mean to tell me that your own uncle took you to a place where you were hung upside-down on a cross and men and women drugged and raped you? Whatever!" or "You expect me to believe that they used, whatever you called it, to control and program you and you have a tracking device in your head?" or "I'm supposed to believe your own dad made you watch while he murdered your baby sister?" It is a very wounding thing to be so traumatized and violated and no one will believe you. So they shut themselves inside forever or until one day, they may find a soul they can talk to that will really hear them and give them a chance to vent, grieve and heal in an atmosphere of loving acceptance. What would the Lord do? Are you indeed His representative? He who has ears to hear, let him hear!

What Happens in Vegas STAYS in Vegas!

It shouldn't have to be said, but I'll say it anyway. No matter what someone shares with you or how juicy the details, it needs to be held in the utmost confidence. I believe that the discretion of a minister is oftentimes more crucial than that of the lawyer/client privilege. Someone is opening up their soul to tell you all of the sordid accounts of their life and is trusting you with it. I have seen times in ministry where keeping this confidence is quite literally a matter of life and death, especially when someone has either enemies or abusers that have threatened them or they have suicidal or self harming tendencies.

Under no circumstance would I suggest you share things with anyone else without their permission and even then, someone that dissociates may not be able to make a good decision whether or not to grant permission in their fragile state of mind.

There can be advantages to ministering with a partner and I would recommend you to do so if you know someone you can trust and the person receiving ministry is comfortable with that, but that ministry partner should be there from the beginning and kept abreast of the happenings going on in the sessions they are not present in. This can be a tag team effort when done this way. By the way, not including a partner, especially in face-to-face encounters can be ministry suicide, especially for male ministers.

KNOWING HEAVEN BACKS YOU

It is important to understand that heaven backs you and why heaven backs you. The answer is quite simple yet profound. It's because God cares for you, yes, YOU! His love for you is without measure. To prove this, I will let the Word of God speak for itself.

Romans 8:37-39 Yet in all these things we are more than conquerors through Him who loved us. For I am persuaded that neither death nor life, nor angels nor principalities nor powers, nor things present nor things to come, nor height nor depth, nor any other created thing, shall be able to separate us from the love of God which is in Christ Jesus our Lord.

Settle it in your heart. God is your Father that loves you more than you can comprehend. Not only that, He promises to take care of you and meet your daily needs.

Matthew 6:25-33 Therefore I say to you, do not worry about your life, what you will eat or what you

will drink; nor about your body, what you will put on. Is not life more than food and the body more than clothing? Look at the birds of the air, for they neither sow nor reap nor gather into barns; yet your heavenly Father feeds them. Are you not of more value than they? Which of you by worrying can add one cubit to his stature?

"So why do you worry about clothing? Consider the lilies of the field, how they grow: they neither toil nor spin; and yet I say to you that even Solomon in all his glory was not arrayed like one of these. Now if God so clothes the grass of the field, which today is, and tomorrow is thrown into the oven, *will He* not much more *clothe* you, O you of little faith?

"Therefore do not worry, saying, 'What shall we eat?' or 'What shall we drink?' or 'What shall we wear?' For after all these things the Gentiles seek. For your heavenly Father knows that you need all these things. But seek first the kingdom of God and His righteousness, and all these things shall be added to you.

Notice, it doesn't read, "But seek AFTER the doctor said you're gonna die, the lawyer says you're going to lose everything, or when you realize all hope is gone." It says to seek Him FIRST, AND His righteousness! It is important to be in right standing with Him. Nor does it say, "SOME of these things MIGHT be added unto you". It reads ALL these things SHALL be added to you. God is not our last resort, He is our first defense! He also wants to handle your problems for you.

1 Peter 5:6-7 Therefore humble yourselves under

the mighty hand of God, that He may exalt you in due time, casting all your care upon Him, for He cares for you.

What else does He want for you?

3 John 2 Beloved, I wish above all things that thou mayest prosper and be in health, even as thy soul prospereth. (KJV)

Above ALL things, He wants you to succeed, to have your needs met, to be healthy and happy. Sounds like what any good father would want for his child. What about your future?

Jeremiah 29:11 For I know the thoughts that I think toward you, says the Lord, thoughts of peace and not of evil, to give you a future and a hope.

Now that we have established that God loves you, wants to take care of you, wants to handle your cares, that He wants you to be healthy, happy and to succeed and that He has plans for you, you can know why heaven backs you. Let's look deeper and see that heaven is set and ready to back and equip you.

We know, from the very first verses of the Bible that God created the heavens and the earth.(**Genesis 1**) If you were to read the first chapter of the Bible, you would see that God spoke the world into existence. He said, **"Let there be light"** and there was light, then He saw it and said it was good. He continued calling things into being with His words until the world was there before His eyes. He didn't have to sweat and toil, wipe His brow, or ask some angels to fetch Him some water. He simply spoke, knowing what He said would come to pass. Then, He was ready for His masterpiece...

Genesis 1:26-27 Then God said, "Let Us make man in Our image, according to Our likeness; let them have dominion over the fish of the sea, over the birds of the air, and over the cattle, over all the earth and over every creeping thing that creeps on the earth." So God created man in His image; in the image of God He created him; male and female He created them.

Two things to note. Man was created in the image of God. When the Father looked at man, He saw Himself, just like any other proud dad. He made us to have dominion over the earth. He gave us authority over the earth and we, like Him, speak our own world into existence every day. What you say and expect to happen is what you will see. It is important to speak what you want. Have you ever noticed that the person that complains about living paycheck to paycheck and barely gets by, never gets ahead? What about the one that claims that their family gets the flu every year? The whole family gets an awful case like clockwork every year because they expect to have what they say, good or bad. I'd rather boast about how good God provides for me, how I walk in divine health and how blessed my family is and expect that to be my reality. Have you ever heard the expression, a man is as good as his word? His or her life is as good as their words.

Our home here on earth, our surroundings, those around us and what happens around us day to day is what is called the natural realm; life as we know it and experience it with our senses. No two people experience the same things, are surrounded by the same people or circumstances and are truly unique to anyone else that has ever lived. Think of how special you are!

Co-existing with the natural realm is the spiritual realm. The spiritual realm created the natural one and is just as real and even more essential. The natural world we see and experience with our senses is a temporary state, but who and what you really are, which is a spirit, is eternal. God is Spirit and He created man in His own image. First, we are spirit, the part of us that comes out of God, Himself. We have a soul which consists of personalities, our preferences, our emotions and our talents; what makes you uniquely you. In order for God to place us here in the natural realm, we needed a vehicle to move around in; our earth suit or body. We are a spirit that has a soul and lives in a body. Our spirit is the eternal part of us.

2 Corinthians 4:18 While we do not look at the things which are seen, but at the things which are not seen. For the things which are seen *are* temporary, but the things which *are* not seen are eternal.

So how far back do you go within the spiritual realm? Far before your birth date.

Ephesians 1:3-12 Blessed *be* the God and Father of our Lord Jesus Christ, who has blessed us with every spiritual blessing in the heavenly *places* in Christ, just as He chose us in Him before the foundation of the world, that we should be holy and

without blame before Him in love, having predestined us to adoption as sons by Jesus Christ to Himself, according to the good pleasure of His will, to the praise of the glory of His grace, by which He made us accepted in the Beloved.

In Him we have redemption through His blood, the forgiveness of sins, according to the riches of His grace which He made to abound toward us in all wisdom and prudence, having made known to us the mystery of His will, according to His good pleasure which He purposed in Himself, that in the dispensation of the fullness of the times He might gather together in one all things in Christ, both which are in heaven and which are on earth—in Him. In Him also we have obtained an inheritance, being predestined according to the purpose of Him who works all things according to the counsel of His will, that we who first trusted in Christ should be to the praise of His glory.

Jeremiah 1:5 Before I formed you in the womb I knew you; Before you were born I sanctified you; I ordained you a prophet to the nations.

You and God go way back! Before you were formed in your mother's womb, even before the foundations of the world, He knew you. The Word of God is filled with promises for YOU! God wants you to walk in those promises and grow in them. Here are just a few...

Matthew 7:7 Ask, and it will be given to you; seek, and you will find; knock, and it will be opened to you.

John 14:13-14 And whatever you ask in My name, that I will do, that the Father may be glorified in the Son. If you ask anything in My name, I will do *it*.

Matthew 21:22 And whatever things you ask in prayer, believing, you will receive.

Sounds like a fairytale. What about the part where the wolf is at the door huffing and puffing to blow our house down? I'm glad you asked. Let's look at another scripture. In **John 10:10** It says, **The thief does not come except to steal, and to kill, and to destroy**. BUT Jesus said, **I have come that they may have life, and that they may have it more abundantly**. Let me put it this way, if it is trying to steal anything from you, from material things to your peace of mind; if it is trying to kill you, by an accident or sickness or if it is trying to destroy you, your life, your family or your reputation, IT'S NOT OF GOD! Jesus came so you might have life and that more abundantly! God is not the one trying to take from you. His very nature is to GIVE and LOVE! So what about the enemy? What do I do about that? That's a great question! As it turns out, Jesus took care of that already. From Abraham we see God's promise to his descendents.

Genesis 22:17 ...blessing I will bless you, and multiplying I will multiply your descendants as the stars of the heaven and as the sand which *is* on the seashore; and your descendants shall possess the gate of their enemies.

Luke 10:19 Behold, I give you the authority to trample on serpents and scorpions, and over all the power of the enemy, and nothing shall by any means hurt you.

Mark 16:15-18 And He said to them, "Go into all the world and preach the gospel to every creature. He who believes and is baptized will be saved; but he who does not believe will be condemned. And these signs will follow those who believe: In My name they will cast out demons; they will speak with new tongues; they will take up serpents; and if they drink anything deadly, it will by no means hurt them; they will lay hands on the sick, and they will recover.

Matthew 8:16 When evening had come, they brought to Him many who were demon-possessed. And He cast out the spirits with a word, and healed <u>ALL</u> who were sick.

As you can see in scripture, God loves you and wants what's best for you. He has plans for you and has known you since long before you were born. He created you in His own image and has you in a place of dominion in this world and has given you authority over the enemy. Heaven has your back! As you minister to others or even to yourself, have confidence in that. Say what you want to come to pass and say those words with authority in Christ and just watch what God will do through you!

FOUR DIRECTION FORGIVENESS

Matthew 6:14-15 reads, For if you forgive men their trespasses, your heavenly Father will also forgive you, But if you do not forgive men their trespasses, neither will your Father forgive your trespasses.

The Bible is quite clear about forgiveness. We must forgive as God has forgiven us and if we choose not to forgive others, He chooses to refrain from forgiving us. The Father lays the law down on this one, not to enforce a rule, but because of the poison unforgiveness brings to one's life. The person you can't forgive still holds power over you, or I should say, takes power from you. In order to heal completely, forgiveness must take place.

The carnal nature of man, the flesh, when it has been abused, hurt or misused wants to lash out, strike back, plot revenge and broil in bitterness and anger or hatred. When something wicked to inflict pain or damage has been intentionally done to you or someone you love, the decision to forgive becomes a hard one and yet, God instructs us to do so. He wouldn't call on us to do it, if He won't equip us to do it.

Forgiveness is not some kind of mental assent. It is a decision and a heart action. It is not playing games with the mind, simply trying to forget an offense, making light of it, or being in a state of denial.

Hebrews 8:12 For I will be merciful to their unrighteousness, and their sins and their lawless deeds I will remember no more.

We have already established that we must forgive to have God's forgiveness, therefore, the verse of **Hebrews 8:12** would apply to one that chooses to walk in forgiveness. He says He will be merciful, or forgive, unrighteousness, sins and iniquities and then will remember them no more. That means that forgiving comes before forgetting, not the other way around. True forgiveness can cause you to forget the pain of the past, but trying to forget first does not lead to real and healing forgiveness.

Ephesians 4:26-27 "Be angry, and do not sin": Do not let the sun go down on your wrath, nor give place to the devil.

It is permissible to be angry, but not to stay angry. It might seem justifiable to stay angry, bitter and concoct delicious revenge in your mind, but that isn't the way to peace and wholeness, no matter the temptation. The Bible says in **Romans 8:6-7. For to be carnally minded *is* death, but to be spiritually minded *is* life and peace. Because the carnal mind *is* enmity against God; for it is not subject to the law of God, nor indeed can be.**

It is clear that the carnal man sees things much differently, if not completely opposite of how God sees them.

Isaiah 55:8-9 "For My thoughts *are* not your thoughts, Nor *are* your ways My ways," says the Lord. 9 "For *as* the heavens are higher than the earth, So are My ways higher than your ways, And My thoughts than your thoughts.

Just as true forgiveness is not a matter of the mind, it is also not something one can just declare to be so and hope that will suffice. It is a position of the heart, not a feeling, but a choice. God sees into the heart. The Word says in **Luke 6:45 ...For out of the abundance of the heart his mouth speaks.**

Speaking alone doesn't change a heart unless there is a willingness to change.

1 John 2:9-10 He who says he is in the light, and hates his brother, is in darkness until now. He who loves his brother abides in the light, and there is no cause for stumbling in him.

Forgiveness isn't about excusing or condoning what was done to you. It's not about belittling the harm done, nor pretending it didn't happen. It's not about giving in or even giving up your justification to be angry. It's not about submitting to someone that hurt you or going along to get along even with a fear of recurrence.

Forgiveness is about making a decision to move forward and to not look back; to release the other person so you're no longer tied to them. To cut cords to the weights that are trying to drown you. It's the refusal to continue to relive the past trauma over and over in your thoughts. It's a choice to let go so you can reach for something else, something new. To decide to use your energy and motivation to be better and not bitter; to decide to start anew.

The Lord showed me as I was praying about this, that there are four directions of forgiveness. They may not all apply to each offense, but I would encourage you to check each one before brushing it off and negating it. The first and most obvious, is to forgive the perpetrator, the one whose face you see when you picture the event on the screen of your mind. There may be more than one person that comes to mind, but I suggest you do this in a systematic way and process this one step at a time. Whether or not you know their name, or even what they look like; as sometimes the offender is masked, hidden or disguised, it is imperative that you truly forgive them.

The second direction of forgiveness is toward any person or people, that in some way contributed to the traumatic occurrence whether they were physically present at the time or not. This could be any accessory to the crime, a participant of the ritual, someone that viewed or filmed the incident without helping or interceding, a handler that did the programming, the executive that had overseen the transaction, the one that profited from the harm that was inflicted, the one that knew the secret, but never told or went for help, the parent that turned their head and allowed it to happen, anyone that was gratified sexually or financially from that torment, etc.. As you can see, because every trauma is unique and all of the characters and scenes are different, the possibilities are like snowflakes. One must look at each circumstance and identify each person in which it is necessary to release and forgive. As time progresses, the Lord may bring others to mind that need to be forgiven. This may be a process that needs to be worked through, but take heart, progress is moving forward even if it comes in stages.

The third direction of forgiveness is toward oneself. What? How can that be, that the victim needs to forgive themselves? How may times have you beaten yourself up about something that happened to you? Keep in mind that an abuser often places blame on the one being abused and especially in a young, confused or shattered mind, they often receive that blame into their heart. Their mind might play the IF ONLY game with them; "If only I hadn't broken that, then Daddy wouldn't have gotten so mad", "If only I hadn't worn that outfit or went to that place", "If only I hadn't gone in that car", "If only I hadn't got sucked into to that","If only I hadn't pursued fame", "If only I hadn't tried that drug", "If only I hadn't murdered my own child",...IF ONLY is a hellish game that could go on forever and ends up nowhere. Only pain, shame and regret are there. We must see ourselves as God sees us and the value He placed in each of us. We must shut down the lies our own minds try to condemn us with. Forgiving oneself may be the hardest thing, but must be done in order to put the past where it belongs.

No matter what you have done, God can forgive whatever it is and even forget it. David not only committed adultery, but then committed murder to cover it up, yet God said that David was a man after God's own heart. Paul persecuted and murdered Christians and yet ended up writing at least eight books, and some scholars believe up to thirteen books of the Bible. The Word is full of stories of people that had character flaws that God used in profound ways. He can turn your tragedy into triumph and wants to, because He loves you dearly. If He can forgive you, I propose that you can and should forgive yourself. The Word says that **if a house is divided against itself, that house cannot stand. (Mark 3:25)** If you are against your own self, how can you expect to stand? The blood of Jesus is powerful enough to wash away ALL sin, even yours.

The fourth and final direction of our forgiveness needs to be toward God, Himself. Yes, but He is good and perfect and can do no wrong. You are absolutely right to think that, however, He sure does get blamed for a lot. Remember, it is the thief that comes to steal, kill and destroy, not God. If it has tried to steal from you, including your health, finances, peace, relationships or your joy, to kill you or destroy you, it is not of God, but of the enemy of your soul. Jesus said that He has come to give you life and that more abundantly. If you can't see your life as abundant, then you aren't walking in all that He has for you. We live in a fallen world and sadly God is blamed and hated for it. Let's look at another scripture. One so familiar that it often gets overlooked.

John 3:16-17 For God so loved the world that He gave His only begotten Son, that whoever believes in Him should not perish but have everlasting life. For God did not send His Son into the world to condemn the world, but that the world through Him might be saved.

For God SO loved the world, He gave His ONLY begotten Son. Let's stop right there. Look at it again and absorb it into your spirit. Imagine having your pride and joy, your beloved child, your only son and GIVING that son for a flawed and sinful world. Can you imagine what kind of love it would take to give a perfect son for you? His love is so great, it is incomprehensible, yet He chooses to give it willingly and freely. By not seeing God as a loving Father, we, in essence, are placing blame on Him for our circumstances. He is often blamed for the loss of life, love and property, though it is not Him that steals from us. How many times have you heard someone say that He must have needed that child in heaven? The words are sweetened but place blame on Him just the same. Even natural disasters are referred to as "Acts of God", yet we see in the Bible that Jesus calmed the storms.

We must sincerely examine our hearts to see if we need to forgive God. Although He has done nothing wrong, we must forgive Him of our perception of wrongdoing or neglect. We not only need to forgive Him, but we need to make peace in our hearts toward Him and ask Him for His forgiveness for the perceived offenses we wrongfully held against Him.

Yes, but you don't understand what has happened to me and how horrific it was. You don't understand how damaged and broken I am. You don't get what I've done. I can never forgive myself. I have a right to my anger. Yes, you do. You are justified in your anger and pain. I'm not minimizing that, but you can choose to let go of that which torments and is killing you. It is your choice. The Lord tells us we must forgive to receive forgiveness from Him. He instructs us from His position of Love.

What if it was so long ago that you'd have no idea how to find the person, the person is dead, or you'd be put in harm's way to see them or you are certain that they wouldn't care or respond anyway?

Here is what the Word says in **Matthew 18:15 Moreover if your brother sins against you, go and tell him his fault between you and him alone. If he hears you, you have gained your brother.** This scripture gives direction concerning resolving a conflict with a brother in Christ. It isn't necessarily a matter that is advisable to handle in person or face to face otherwise. True forgiveness is always a matter of the heart and starts there. The Lord may impress upon you to contact someone to resolve an issue at some point, but your willingness and heart must be in it or it is of no benefit.

You may know you must forgive and even want to, but can't seem to get beyond the pain and hurt to truly forgive. What then? Here is the most wonderful part. You aren't expected to do this alone. You aren't alone. All of the benefits of the Kingdom of God are not done by man, but through man by God Almighty. Can a man give life to himself apart from God? Can man save himself, heal, deliver or even raise the dead apart from Him? Absolutely not! We rely on Him for all of it. When we receive Christ, we become dead to self so we can take on His life through us. He is our Salvation, our Healer, our Deliverer. our Shelter, our Peace, our Joy, our Provider, He is I AM. When we acknowledge His attributes, He shows up with what we need at that moment. He forgives us, therefore we can forgive others. He enables us to do so. Where we are weak, He shows Himself strong on our behalf. All you have to do is ask Him to help you to truly forgive, to see the situation from His perspective, and to forgive from your heart. Ask Him to take the pain, anger, shame, the torment or anything else that stands between you and letting it go. Know that if you ask Him to help you with a sincere heart, He will hear and answer you. Let it go and let God be God. You may have never been able to trust or count on anyone before, but you CAN put your trust in Him now. He will never leave you nor forsake you.

As a fractured soul begins to heal, more memories and events come to the surface that will need to be forgiven, but healing can begin here. It may not fix everything and make that person completely whole, but it is crucial to the process. As memories surface, this step will need to be visited again and again. Keep this in mind as you minister.

Science has proven that stress impacts our health in a tremendous way. Some articles cite that over 90% of diseases can be traced back to stress as its cause. When someone has been so wronged and harmed emotionally, it takes its toil on the body. Unforgiveness, resentment, bitterness, pent up rage or anger, hatred and self hatred contribute to the toxic mix within the body. Self hatred is the main cause of auto-immune diseases in which the body attacks itself, mimicking the soul's self loathing till it manifests in the body. One can choose to remain in that quagmire or they can command those things to leave in the name of Jesus. I will make the assumption that you would want to be rid of those things, so I'll ask that you read the following out loud, believing that when you give these commands in confidence and authority, they will leave. Let's get rid of these hindrances now. Appropriate this to the person you're ministering to or to yourself. In the prayer, as you pray to forgive those that hurt you, go through each individual one at a time. If you know their name, then use it, if you don't, then identify them by what they did. Make sure to include each perpetrator, accomplice or anyone else involved, yourself and God as needed. Anyone that you hold a grudge or resentment toward, even if you feel it is justified. Let it go. Release them one by one. Don't allow anyone to hinder you from moving forward. Go through this process until you are sure that all is forgiven and if you remember anyone else you had forgotten, make sure you come back to this again. It's important.

Father, You know all that has happened to me, everything I've suffered and why I feel the way I do. I know I am supposed to forgive others and want to, but it's not easy for me and I need your help. I have decided I am finished with all of the things that hinder me and attack my mind and body, so in the name of Jesus, I command unforgiveness, resentment, bitterness, rage, anger, hatred, self hatred and loathing to leave me now! Anxiety and stress GO! Do not come back! You are never to return! God, I release it all to You and ask Your help to truly forgive those that have hurt me, including myself. Lord, I forgive my perpetrator _____ for _____, I forgive each accomplice, one by one. I forgive _____ for _____. I forgive myself for_____. Lord, I forgive You for_____. I repent of unforgiveness and ask You to forgive me for ever holding any in my heart. I now let go of the thoughts that have tormented me. I command my body to be healed and my emotional pain to be healed NOW! Lord, I place the injustices done to me in Your hands and trust You to right the wrongs against me. Thank You, Lord for Your love and help and for being with me through this. Amen.

DEALING WITH FEAR

Just as being burnt causes us to avoid a hot iron or being hurt in a fall makes one leery of heights, trauma creates fear and apprehension. We naturally avoid the things that harm us. One that has suffered great abuses can become so full of fear, they can barely function. Relating to others can be very difficult. Trusting anyone can sometimes be impossible. It is easier to go it alone and push others away than it is to let people in, particularly if those that should have been able to be trusted has betrayed you. When you have those that show concern and love in the open and then become abusers behind closed doors, you learn there is no one you can feel safe around or trust and to guard your heart at all costs. Life can be very confusing if the world you live in is like a continual earthquake where you never have firm footing and you wonder what will fall on you next. Sometimes the escape is to hide in a compartment of the mind and allow your psyche to alter at will.

Fear can cripple and hinder a person. Fear can be the natural reaction to what has occurred or it can be used to intentionally control, manipulate or blackmail someone. It can be a real or perceived threat and still have the same power over its victim. Fear can shut down the senses as though you're paralyzed and unable to breathe. It can keep you from speaking out, standing up for yourself or moving forward. Fear can be a spirit, but is often a very strong emotion and can be a stronghold of the mind. It is often said that fear is the opposite of faith, but faith is a choice to trust and believe. The opposite of faith is unbelief. The opposite of fear is security. Out of security comes peace, confidence and a sense of calm. Feelings are temporal. They are subject to change. We have authority over the spirit of fear and can command it to leave.

1 John 4:18 There is no fear in love; but perfect love casts out fear: because fear involves torment. But he who fears has not been made perfect in love.

This verse says that perfect love casts out fear. Some of the stories I've heard would indicate that many people have never known or felt love. We must show them love and compassion and share the love of the Father with them. Prayerfully, that can happen in a blink of an eye, but be prepared that sometimes it takes a while and we must not give up. That person in front of you or in your mirror that is so wounded needs to know and feel real love. Keep reaching out! For God so loved the world, He gave and as He is, so are we in this world. Believe and know you are loved.

Matthew 10:26 Therefore do not fear them. For there is nothing covered that will not be revealed, and hidden that will not be known.

You may, like me, have once been someone's dirty little secret, but the Word says that those hidden things will eventually be revealed and you needn't be a prisoner to fear any longer. Fear can take on many forms like anxiety, worry or stress. There may be many things in which to be afraid, but that can end right now. There are well over a hundred verses in the Bible that encourage us not to fear and to be not afraid. God doesn't want us to be tormented and hindered. If you are ready to take a stand against fear, pray these words out loud and with great confidence that heaven is backing what you say.

Father, I thank you for loving me and I receive Your perfect love. In Jesus name, I command all oppression, hindrances, torment, nightmares, worry, stress, anxiety and fear of all types, fear of recurrence, fear of death, fear of the future, fear of men, fear of the unknown, fear of governments, fear of failure, fear of punishment, fear of threats, blackmail, witchcraft, and any other demonic activity must GO NOW, never to return! No weapon formed against me will prosper and I thank you Lord for peace and security within me that sustains me and for Your protection and provision. Amen!

DISCOVERING SELF WORTH

Many years ago I visited an art exhibit and was so impressed with the pieces on display. There were sculptures and paintings with such intricate details and stunning colors that some even touched my emotions. Then I turned the corner and saw something that I didn't expect. I saw two square frames. Both had a stark white background, and in one was a solid red circle right in the middle that was about four inches in diameter. The other had a plain red square painted in the center, about four inches on each side. Frankly, I felt like a kindergartener that could color within the lines could have made both of them in under five minutes if they had paper and red paint. Out of sheer curiosity, I looked for the price and was shocked. They were ticketed at well over $1000 each and were marked higher than some of the other pieces there. When the guide saw me looking at the price, she inquired if I was interested in purchasing them and I commented that I wondered why they were so expensive. She retorted that the value of something was reflected in what someone was willing to pay for it. Although I felt like those paintings would sit there a very long time or were at some point going to be drastically reduced, she had a very valid point. It could also be that the artist and creator of those paintings now has them proudly adorning the walls in his own home, but they do have value.

Psalm 139:14 I will praise You, for I am fearfully *and* wonderfully made; Marvelous are Your works, And *that* my soul knows very well.

Did you know that you were created with love and great care? He shaped you, colored you and made you unique and special from anyone else. Want to know what you're worth? He paid for YOU with the precious life of His Son. He adores you and wants you as His own!

Anyone that has suffered some sort of abuse has become an object of some kind whether it be a punching bag, an outhouse, a sexual plaything, a toy, a pawn, a weapon or an amusement. Objects are made to be used by someone and are often tossed away when they are done. Although you may have been made to feel like an object, please know that you are NOT one! I am very sorry for what has happened to you, but please know that it's time to take your life back. You have great value, are very loved and are created for a purpose.

There is an old adage that reads, "Sticks and stones may break my bones, but words will never harm me." What a crock! Long after the physical wounds are healed the words still bite. Words are chosen to intimidate, to belittle, to hurt, to shame and to stifle the soul. Opponents talk smack on the field all the time knowing it gets under the skin and affects the performance of the other players. A drill instructor even uses words in such a way to make soldiers submit. An abuser uses it to control. If they can make the victim fear, feel weak or useless, they don't get as much of a fight. Words can harm and can even kill if they are believed and embraced. Lies can be deadly, but lies aren't truth. God has not forgotten you or your value.

Isaiah 49:15-16 Can a woman forget her nursing child, And not have compassion on the son of her womb? Surely, they may forget, yet I will not forget you. See, I have inscribed you on the palms of My hands; Your walls are continually before Me.

A few years back, one of my co-workers and I were having a conversation as he was leaving for the day. He was loading down his wheelchair and was very excited to be leaving work. I asked him if he had any plans that evening and he said he was going out to celebrate. I asked him what was the occasion and he replied, "I'm celebrating the sixteenth year anniversary of my accident!" I asked, "You celebrate that?" and Carl said, "You bet I do! I survived!" Some question whether a glass is half full or half empty and Carl was celebrating his glass! That really blessed me. He wasn't agonizing over the injury and how it changed his life, he wasn't going out to sulk and cry in his beer, but he made plans to go out and celebrate that he was still here to talk about it. I love that!

If you're reading this right now, guess what? You survived too! You were strong enough to make it and that calls for a celebration in itself! You are strong enough to withstand what you didn't deserve and you have the power within yourself to start anew. What happened to you was a crime! It was not your fault! You aren't to blame! You may have been made to feel shame, rejection, worthless, useless, condemned and maybe a thousand other things but you were made to feel that way. Feelings are temporal. That isn't who you are. You were a victim, and it's time to become a victor. Reject those damning thoughts that negate you in any way. You are loved. You are special. You are strong. You have the strength and ability to accept and love yourself and to start over.

Let's try an exercise. In your mind only, start hearing the ABCs. Keep going as you continue to read. A,B,C,D,E,F,G... NOW, start counting out loud with your voice. 1,2,3,4,5... What happened to the alphabet in your mind when you spoke out the numbers? It stopped, huh? Your thoughts quieted so you could hear what you were saying. Even your own mind is designed to stop and listen to your own words. I want to encourage you to start speaking the truth out loud if negative thoughts come to your mind and watch your life change. It doesn't matter if you have to do it ten times a minute at first, counteract your negative thoughts with positive words and if you can find a Bible verse to support it, that's even better. If a thought comes to you that you're "a loser" You might say, "I am a victor in Christ. I am fearfully and wonderfully made". You already know the thoughts you battle. Prepare a positive truth for every one and shut those thoughts down! Reject those negative thoughts and never embrace them again. Let's address this now in prayer. Remember there is power in your words, they create your world.

Father, I thank you that I am a survivor! I thank you for strength and for allowing me escape. Thank you for showing me that what I went through was not my fault and that life is something to be celebrated. In Jesus name, I command every negative word, every curse, all rejection, shame, belittlement, torment, intimidation and emotional pain to leave NOW! I command low self esteem, self sabotage, self harm, self hatred, resentment, bitterness, isolation, anger, murder, cutting and suicidal thoughts to cease and leave NOW in the

name of Jesus. From this moment on, I refuse to entertain any negative thoughts or fear of any kind and instead, will speak positive truth. Lord, help me to find value in myself and also value in others every day. Help me to love myself and to be able to trust others and to accept love from people without pushing them away. Father, help me to become the person you created me to be. Thank you for Your mercy and grace. Amen.

GOT VOICES?

To some degree, everyone has inner voices. Our thoughts speak to us. We all have thoughts that correct, coax or condemn us. Thoughts like, "I really need to go and clean out my closet", "I should have told them no and that I didn't have time", "Wow! Look at his smile, he's cute", "I need to find another job", "You idiot! Why did you do that?" or, "Ugh! I am getting to be so fat!" Woulda, shoulda, coulda thoughts run through our heads all of the time and we hear them from within. God speaks to us too. What He says may be to encourage us, to direct us, or guide us to help someone else. The enemy talks to us as well. He may tempt us, try to distract us, discourage us or attempt to instill fear. He may try to take us off our path, or coax us to say or do something to hurt someone else. All of these voices usually sound like our own voice. After all, our own voice is more convincing and trusted to us than any other.

There can be voices that are heard by our ears that no one else hears. Medically referred to as auditory hallucinations, these voices can be symptoms of various mental disorders such as bipolar disorder and schizophrenia. With these disorders, these auditory hallucinations can be related to psychosis or a loss of reality. The cause of this can be simply related to the dopamine levels in the brain. The voices one hears related to psychosis are usually heard from outside of the person.

Those dealing with dissociation hear voices from within themselves. They are not related to psychosis. They are not caused by a break from reality or a chemical imbalance. These are the voices of alters or parts from within the core person. They can sound very different. They can be young or old, different genders, accents or sound the same. They can talk to the core or among the parts.

When any part of a person's psyche is demonized, which is often the case with SRA or satanic ritual abuse victims, more voices can be layered in, involving demonic commands or suggestions. I have ministered to people at times when I could hear slamming, howling, banging and demonic voices audibly. I can't begin to imagine what it sounds like in their heads.

If the voices heard are from a mental disorder, Jesus provided your healing on the whipping post 2000 years ago. If the voices are coming from demons, you have authority over all the power of the enemy and can make them shut up and leave. As I have prayed about the voices from parts and alters, I saw tiny people in cubicles of the mind, compartmentalized, shouting over the walls to try and talk to one another and then I heard the words, "Dissolve the compartments." I then saw a refiner melting glass pieces back together and again a Refiner refining silver. I believe that this can bring one voice and one mind. NOONE or NOTHING is a lost cause!

Matthew 19:26 But Jesus looked at *them* and said to them, "With men this is impossible, but with God all things are possible."

John 14:13-14 And whatever you ask in My name, that I will do, that the Father may be glorified in the Son. If you ask anything in My name, I will do *it*.

Let's pray and believe. Say this out loud and with confidence that heaven backs you.

In the name of Jesus, I thank you Lord that your Word is true and that I am healed by Your stripes. I command my dopamine levels to be perfect for my body for optimum health. I command all oppression, tormenting, or familiar spirits, or anything that is not of God to SHUT UP and GET OUT NOW in Jesus name! I command the compartments of my mind to be dissolved and that my voice becomes one. I trust You Lord as my Refiner and Healer of my spirit, soul and body to make me whole. I declare Your Peace and Comfort is within me and I can yield to You. You made me and You can remake me and heal my mind and soul. I declare it is done now. In Jesus name I pray, Amen.

CONCERNING DEMONS

Not everyone that dissociates is plagued with demons, however in some instances, the one that comes to steal, kill and destroy takes opportunities to torment and oppress the soul of a person. Whether demons are invoked in rituals, in programming or come to simply pounce on someone's weak state, it becomes necessary to address the enemy and cast it out. I don't suggest looking for devils, but we are to be mindful of his tactics. In the following scripture, note again the importance of forgiveness.

2 Corinthians 2:10-11 Now whom you forgive anything, I also *forgive*. For if indeed I have forgiven anything, I have forgiven that one for your sakes in the presence of Christ, lest Satan should take advantage of us; for we are not ignorant of his devices.

I can only share with you from my own experiences in ministry. Although I've done lots of research to look for answers in order to minister to others, I have found that the guidance from Holy Spirit throughout the process in different circumstances and what I have learned through trial and error is what has taught me the most.

As I have had conversations with alters, I have found that they know who I am and relate to me. Some may address me more formally than others or even present different attitudes while speaking to me, but I don't have to introduce myself to each one. Some like me, and some don't. Because the core knows me, they seem to as well. Demons, on the other hand, will often ask, "Who are you?" or "Who do you think you are?" They often use foul language and have called me some choice names. They can sound different, smell different and look different and usually don't like you if they know you can make them go away. They have no interest in relating to you, only in trying to scare, belittle or threaten. If you know who you are in Christ, their bark is far worse than their bite. There is something about the righteousness of Christ, in that you can stand before God without guilt and before any demon or sickness without fear. They have to obey you in the name of Jesus.

One night, the wee hours of the morning actually, I was awakened by a phone call and, half asleep, I am listening to what I can only describe as a parade of alters. I was hearing different accents, names, ages...you name it,... then I heard fear. As I began to get my bearings, I started to command fear and its cause to go in Jesus name and suddenly this very gravelly, guttural, evil voice started calling me some names I won't share here, then asked, "Who do you think you are, you @#$+ ?" Then I was suddenly wide awake and angry! I said, "I am a child of the Living God and you need to shut up and get out NOW in Jesus name!" I heard some yelling and protest and then it was gone. I called the core's name and he mentioned being sleepy and that was that.

Demons can be seen, heard or detected in the room as well as within the person's soul. The little twits can cause physical harm to a person, although that is somewhat rare. One young woman had to go to the hospital with very deep claw marks that looked like they were made by some kind of animal straight down her back from her neck to lower back. They could not be explained. Some demons can cause a person to cut themselves or even to commit suicide. I know of several instances in which people I have ministered to have tried killing themselves. It has been explained to me that the marks one leaves on their body like dots, lines and dashes while cutting, mutilating themselves or causing self harm can sometimes be read like some sort of demonic code. I have also seen people cut words, pentagrams and numbers in their flesh.

Demons can force someone to astral travel. Astral travel or astral projection involves some sort of out of body experience seemingly connected with the second heaven or the demonic realm. I am personally aware at least two instances where that has happened by force, although some partake in astral travel at will. Demons can terrorize a person in their dreams. I know of a man that used drugs to stay awake because of the torment he had while sleeping. After addressing it with ministry he now sleeps like a baby and sometimes reports having godly dreams. Demons also can rape or seduce a person, trying to make their mark or claim. I have known it to be used to cause fear and the act can be very violent. Other times the seduction is seemingly loving and manipulative producing a "spirit husband or wife" causing confusion, division and can really mess with a person's mind.

When the core person detects demonic activity, it has

been my experience that they will usually alter and oftentimes the alter that surfaces shares what they see or hear and what is going on with them. It is often the alter of the youngest age or the one that has been around the longest that reports this. That alter may cry or scream in fear. At that point, it becomes necessary to address the demon directly and command it to leave in Jesus name. I usually encourage the alter to command the demons to leave, but that is not always successful. I will always try to get the core or any alter to stand up to demonic attacks as I want to make them aware that they have the power to do so. If or when demons argue, protest, or try to carry on a conversation, just as Jesus did, we can command them to be quiet and come out in the name of Jesus.

For a period of time, a few months as I recall, I received a phone call nearly every night and could hear little else but screaming over the phone. I started making commands for the attack to stop and after a while a baby alter I could barely hear would whisper in fear and say things to indicate she was hurt, "Owwie, Ms. Meddie! It hurts. They want me to go with them. Make them stop. I don't want to go" amidst more screams. I would stay on the phone with her during the battle until either the core returned to the surface or she fell asleep after I sang to her in the spirit. Many a night I tag-teamed with a ministry partner with this young and highly demonized women that was a victim of satanic ritual abuse. I would get on Skype with the other minister as I had my speakerphone on. We took turns commanding while the other was praying and leaning into Holy Spirit for direction. When I was at work or she couldn't reach me, she'd call the other minister. We kept each other abreast of the day or night's events and it was so helpful to have the help as it was exhausting. Day and night, it was a crazy couple of months for sure! The young woman kept getting pulled back into the cult in a number of ways or it wouldn't have been as drawn out of a process as it was.

Over time, you will learn ways to distinguish the differences between alters and demons. It is important to understand that alters and fragments are part of the individual and are not demons. To try and address an alter as a demon, as something that doesn't belong and to try and cast it out can add insult to injury. We are to heal and make people whole. We aren't to treat them or any part of them like a devil to cast off. Alters can appear as demons and demons like alters, but they are not the same. Also, individual alters can be demonized and we must separate the core person and all his humanity from any demonic activity.

Matthew 10:1 And when He had called His twelve disciples to *Him,* He gave them power *over* unclean spirits, to cast them out, and to heal all kinds of sickness and all kinds of disease.

We have been given power over evil spirits and sickness and disease in Christ. To command evil spirits or demons to come out of someone, even oneself, is called deliverance. Deliverance is often made to seem complicated when it is really very simple. You tell them they have to leave and they leave. The word spirit, in Latin is spiritus, meaning breath. Oftentimes when spirits leave they will do so through the mouth via yawning, burping, coughing or vomiting. Spirits can manifest and get stirred up in other ways, but the majority tend to leave by mouth. It might briefly be uncomfortable, but the freedom is more than worth it. Any commands given need to be verbal and be heard by the one to whom you are ministering. Although I have heard about instances where there was deliverance through worship or prayer cloths, I refer to Jesus' examples and He gave direct commands to the devils to flee and that is what I do.

Throughout this book there are prayers that, if you are participating along, you have already been commanding various things to leave. When I pray deliverance for someone that has alters and fragments, I usually give them an indication as to what to expect; that I will be leaning on Holy Spirit to help with the process, that I will be speaking to the demons directly and what to expect as demons manifest. I comfort them by letting them know that there is nothing to fear and then get their approval to begin. I also suggest applying the blood of Jesus over them and all of their parts. Demons hate the blood, so I have no problem applying it on them too. Here is a sample prayer to pray. Speak boldly with the expectation that what you say will come to pass.

Father, I thank You in advance for what is about to happen. Holy Spirit, I acknowledge You and give You free rule and reign right now, as You want me set free more than even I do. I apply the blood of Jesus over me and to all of the parts of my humanity and I pray a wall be drawn to separate the soul from any demonic presence or anything not of You, Lord. In the name of Jesus, I command spirits of trauma, rejection, shame, fear, torment, oppression and witchcraft to GO NOW! I command mind binding spirits, spirits of mind control, self harm, mutilation, suicide, lying spirits, spirits of death, addiction, depression, anxiety, infirmity, lack, poverty, isolation and strife to leave NOW in Jesus name! I break any satanic ritual, ungodly promise, satanic blood covenant or oath by the power of the

Holy Spirit NOW! I command any demonic or evil spirit or ANYTHING not of God to shut up and get out NOW in Jesus name, never to return! Father, I ask that you fill me full of Your Love, because perfect love casts out all fear. Fill me full of Your Joy, because the Joy of the Lord is my strength and fill me with Your Peace that surpasses all understanding. I ask You to fill me with Your Spirit, Your Comforter and my Helper and Guide in all things and I thank You, Lord for setting me free! Amen.

STAY OUT OF THE WATER

We are doing a lot of work and going through a lot of steps to undo the damage of trauma in all of its forms. I would be remiss if I did not advise you to stay out of the water. What do I mean by that? If you were on the beach and were told that the waters were teaming with hungry sharks and poisonous jellyfish, would you go in? I sure hope not!

We have said that the enemy looks for opportunities. Demons don't play fair and it is best to close all your windows and doors to keep them out. Don't swim in the water, don't wade in it, don't walk in the tide and be careful where you build your sand castles if you catch my drift. Pun intended!

There are things you shouldn't deal with or entertain. We are not to give the devil any place. I'm not going to have you make renunciations, but I will share with you a list of things you may want to avoid...

Any religion that does NOT acknowledge Jesus as having been sent to die for your sins and having rose from the dead, any false god or religion, secret societies like freemasonry, eastern star and shriners, demolay, energy healing, cults, yoga, transcendental meditation, visiting psychics or fortunetellers, palm reading, card reading, crystal balls, playing with ouija boards, dungeons and dragons, seances, new age, calling on the dead, divining for water, black, white or any other color of magic, blood pacts, curses, occult based music, video games or entertainment, astral travel, numerology and consulting horoscopes.

Even if it's not on the list and you think it might be something to avoid, trust your instincts. If in doubt, leave it out.

A number of the items on this list are usually capitalized in written form. The fact that they aren't isn't because something was overlooked in editing. I choose to capitalize every mention of my God or any of His names every chance I get and choose not to give satan, any devil or demonic thing the same honor.

DEVICES OF CONTROL

In some cases of mind control or ritual abuse, various devices are used to control or threaten the victims. Sometimes these are real, sometimes fabricated, but are very effective just the same. For example, an impressionable young child wakes up after being drugged or hypnotized and finds himself covered in blood. He is then told that he has just had "magic surgery". The blood is pretty convincing evidence that a surgery did indeed take place. The child might be told that they have had a bomb placed inside of them that will explode if they were to tell anyone about a killing, ritual or implicate the criminal abuser. They may be told that there is a tracking device implanted in them. Children are often told that they have had a demon or devil's heart placed in them to cause them to do bad things and if they fail to comply with its wishes, it will attack or kill them. These fears often remain with them as they grow into adults and in a very real way, control their minds and actions.

Sometimes real devices are used. Tracking devices or chips can be implanted, oftentimes right behind the ear. Ports can be implanted in the body to administer mind altering drugs. Satanic cobwebs are used in witchcraft to hinder, enslave or demonize their prey. They can be spiritual, but can also be actual cobwebs. They can be used in rituals or the victim may wake up with a cobweb over their face or walk into one unexpectedly, even when entering their car. Demons are invoked in these webs and sometimes they are forcibly made to be swallowed. Pins are also used in rituals upon which demons are attached and then they are usually implanted just under the skin. Pins can be made of slivers of human bone or plastic. The ones I have known that were subjected to this practice had them imbedded around their necks. Poisons can be used with inserts. Dental implants, crystals and a host of other things may be used to track, control, drug, poison, cause fear or demonize a victim. Sometimes these devices can be surgically removed, but God can and has removed them supernaturally.

A few years ago, I had become acquainted with two young ladies that were victims of the same satanic cult. They would watch after and do their best to protect one another. They were like sisters and sought the Lord in their own ways to get out from under the influence of that environment. Both girls had visible pins that could be felt embedded just under the skin around their necks. The youngest shared that her sixteen pins fell to the floor supernaturally while she was worshiping in her Christian church. This report gave me faith for this type of miracle. The older of the two certainly struggled the most as her abuse was more severe. She had thirty-two pins around her neck. Once, in the wee hours of the morning, she called me screaming. Sadly this wasn't at all uncommon at the time. She was being so tormented. These calls would come nightly and were exhausting for me and I can't even fathom what she was going through. I heard banging, like someone locked in a closet was fiercely trying to get out. I heard howling like a wolf and her screaming above it all. Her voice changed to that of a very young girl alter. I was half asleep, trying to calm her and the situation and I started yelling commands for demons to leave and for peace to permeate the room. I remembered about the pins in her neck and decided they had to go. I prayed and asked God, because He loved her and wanted to see her free, to do whatever was necessary to remove them. I asked for angels to be dispersed if needed. In faith, I commanded those pins to dissolve in Jesus name. All of the sudden, it got really quiet and she began to talk in her normal voice. She said, "Ms. Melodie, the pins are gone." I asked her to feel for them to make sure and then instructed her to turn on the lights to check the floor. I know that when dealing with certain satanic relics there are suggested ways to destroy them. My mind was whirling and I didn't want to advise her to gather the demonized pins off the floor, walk them downstairs and just throw them in the dumpster at three in the morning. "No! You don't understand, Ms. Melodie. They are completely gone!"

God is SO good! How amazing is that? God does what no man can do. He does the impossible and He will do it for you and for those that believe! I have included this scripture in the book already, but it bears repeating. **Matthew 19:26 But Jesus looked at *them* and said to them, "With men this is impossible, but with God all things are possible."** When all hope seems lost, you can count on the God of the Impossible. He is able to do anything! We are Christ's representatives in this world and we can believe, command and see miracles to heal and set captives free!

I have just shared with you some testimonies to bolster your faith. Any device, whether from a cult ritual, a handler, programmer or a government intended to control, manipulate, hinder, drug, poison or cripple you in any way can be made harmless, removed or be dissolved supernaturally by the power of the Most High God. Our Father that loves you so much, He sent His Son for YOU. We must believe that He will move on your behalf in this very situation NOW! Let's pray and command with an assurance of His love for you and in faith. Say this out loud with great confidence in Him.

Father, I believe that You love me and want me free. I believe that Jesus came to destroy the works of the enemy. Anything implanted, injected, or fed to me, no matter what it is or made from, will no longer have any effect on me. Right now in Jesus name, I command anything foreign in my body that is not of you to be rendered harmless. That anything placed in me to receive or emit signals of any kind will no longer function. Anything poisonous placed in me will be rendered benign and overcome by the sozo life of God and the rivers of Living Water. Any tracking or controlling device or alien substance of any kind, any chips, ports, pins, webs or any other thing will dissolve NOW! I command any demons attached to flee, never to return in Jesus name! I speak peace, healing, life and restoration from any residual effects to this body and thank You Lord that by His stripes, I am healed! AMEN!

DISSOLVING SOUL TIES

The phrase "soul ties" is not found in the Bible and because of that, some see it as a man-made theory to explain how relationships can impact a person both positively or negatively. I have heard it taught that soul ties are formed during sex. We know that according to the Word in a number of places including, **Genesis 2:24, Matthew 19:5, Mark 10:8** and **Ephesians 5:31**, we see that a **man and his wife become one flesh.** Even in sexual relationships outside of marriage, the Bible speaks of that union as becoming one flesh. Let's have a look.

1 Corinthians 6:16 Or don't you know that he who is joined to a harlot is one body with her? For "the two" He says, **"shall become one flesh."**

In each instance noted above, the sexual act, whether godly or sinful, defines the two becoming one FLESH. Now, Physically, does that mean they become one body? Connected during the act perhaps, but do the two physically meld into one? A child from that union might denote a way in which one flesh could be produced from the two. Even a union with a prostitute, a one night stand, a fleeting encounter without love or commitment produces one flesh from the two according to the Word. Very clearly connections are made during sexual acts.

The types of abuses this book is addressing such as, trauma, SRA, mind control or anything else that can cause dissociation, more often than not, involves forms of sexual crimes. Some are remembered and some are repressed, but I dare say that most of the people I minister to have been abused sexually.

Of course, there are good and healthy relationships and ties our soul has with others. Spouses, children, relatives, friends, teachers, students, neighbors and the like. There are emotional bonds that nourish us and bless our lives. The Bible describes such a relationship so eloquently, as souls being knit together.

1 Samuel 18:1 Now when he had finished speaking to Saul, the soul of Jonathan was knit to the soul of David, and Jonathan loved him as his own soul.

Ungodly or unprofitable relationships can impact a person negatively, even destroying the soul.

Proverbs 6:32 Whoever commits adultery with a woman lacks understanding; He *who* does so destroys his own soul.

There is an interesting phenomenon known as the Stockholm syndrome which is a condition that causes hostages to develop psychological alliances with their captors to survive. Intimate and strong emotional bonds can be formed between two people in spite of danger or risk while one threatens, beats, abuses or intimidates the other. It officially got its name in 1973, when four hostages were taken during a bank robbery in Stockholm, Sweden and the victims refused to testify against their captors. This is also referred to as "capture bonding". Patty Hearst was another famous case of this. She was held hostage by the Symbionese Liberation Army, an urban guerilla group, in 1974 and later denounced her own family and the police. She used a new name, Tania, and ended up working with the SLA to rob corporate banks in San Francisco. In my opinion "Tania" may have been the name of an alter. She publicly expressed sympathetic feelings towards the SLA and their activities. Interestingly enough, after her arrest she tried to plead the Stockholm syndrome as her defense in court. Her seven year prison sentence was commuted and eventually pardoned by Bill Clinton.

    Whether this is a survival tactic, or we want to see the good and humane side of everyone, even our abusers, sometimes unhealthy emotional ties are formed. It is particularly confusing when the abuse comes at the hand of someone you are supposed to trust like a parent, relative, teacher, an authority or even a church member. There are cases when the trauma starts so early in life that the child knows no other way or even understands that it's wrong, let alone that there is hope of anything better. They are simply surviving the best they can, doing what is necessary to win favor, to keep the mistreatment at bay and find themselves continually choosing between the lesser of evils. They thirst for love and acceptance and have no way to find it. God created us in His image and He is Love. Something inside us knows that love is supposed to be in the midst of our being and in our relationships whether we have been loved or not. Life is grossly distorted for some. If that child lives to be old enough, eventually he or she might see that other people have had different lives and backgrounds and may look for love and acceptance if they dare deem themselves worthy of something better.

The importance of forgiveness was covered in a previous chapter. In order to be free from the hold your abuser has over you, forgiveness is key. If you feel that you need to address the topic of forgiveness again, you may want to revisit that chapter and work with God until your heart is free from that burden.

Staying away from your abuser(s) or the environment in which the trauma occurred is strongly advised. Just because a dog returns to its vomit, doesn't mean you have to return to yours. I have known people that have gone back to the same cult that tormented them and I have seen people go back to dangerous relationships. There is a better way and a way of escape and He loves you more than you can imagine.

As you go through this next prayer, I want you to release these people and their ties to you individually. Spend as much time as you need to be thorough. Whether you have one person or sixty people to deal with, cut the ties. Cut them all, one at a time. As you pray, use the name of the person if you know it. If you don't know their name, just tell the Lord, "The person that..., the accomplice, the one that turned their head, the one that knew but didn't do anything to help, the one that filmed it, the person that touched me, that stole this from me, that violated my security....". However you address them, be painstaking in severing each tie. If you are related and have forgiven them, sever this tie emotionally. Sever all bonds to the past that hinder you and be careful about your future relationships. You may not be able to avoid family or certain relationships, but you can control the power they hold over you now and going forward. The most mature thing you can do besides staying free from these entanglements, would be to pray that your abuser(s) might turn their life around and come to the knowledge of Christ for themselves. This prayer may not be easy to do, it's work. I believe that God is there with you to take this burden from you. All you have to do is be willing to give it to Him and ask. Pray this prayer to be free from the bondage of harmful ties. Remember, one person at a time and pray according to each unique situation. Ready? You can do this! Let's break free!

Father, Your Word says that You love me so much that You gave Your only Son for me. I receive Your love and ask for Your help to cut the emotional ties and the pain from those that have hurt or abused me. I want to be free from any harmful tie or connection as well as the torment from my past that has bound me.

Right now, I renounce any connection and cut any tie to (name or identify the person) _____. I have forgiven them for (name the offense) _____ . Before You, Lord, I declare that _____ will no longer have any power over me now or forevermore. I release them in Jesus name.

Father, I also repent from any sexual activity that I have participated in that formed bonds that were not of You and I ask Your forgiveness and I break free from all ties my soul or flesh has made with them. I pray for healing and life in our lives and thank You for healing us and for Your forgiveness.

Lord, according to Your Word, in Luke 6:28, we are to Bless them that curse you, and pray for them which despitefully use you. Therefore, I ask you to bless _____ in every area of his or her life and I pray that _____ will not only turn away from sin, but will no longer hurt anyone else like he or she harmed me. I pray _____will come to the knowledge of Christ and may come to a revelation of Your love for them. Thank you, Lord for setting me free and for blessing and healing me as well as my abuser. In Jesus name I pray, Amen.

ABOUT MEMORIES

Imagine having a computer that crashed on you any number of times, from a few, to several times a day. You never knew when it was going to happen and there was nothing you could do to prevent it. When it came back up, you would have to try to figure out where you left off, if you needed to start over and see what could be restored, discovering some of it was surely lost. You would lose time and become quite frustrated. At some point, you'd decide there was a severe issue with this computer that needed to be addressed. People that dissociate may struggle with their memory in much the same way. Their mind may have glitches that cause them to forget things, whether it be part of their past or a some sort of daily task such as forgetting that the iron was plugged in, failing to pick up the kids or to take medicine. One might lose track of their money or may not remember having heard that a relative had died. When one of these things happen, it may not seem like a big deal, but to the one that battles it every day, it can be quite crippling.

Maybe you try to rely on lists, post-it-notes, strings tied around your finger, items left in plain view or a trusted friend's call to remind yourself of everyday tasks. It could also be that you forget details that are pertinent to your life or maybe scenes of your past or blocks of time are missing from the screen of your mind altogether.

Perhaps you aren't sure if you want all of your memories back. Maybe you fear they might be too painful or vile. Just know that we are asking God's help for this. He is the Healer and can heal those emotions. If there is anything too horrific, we can trust Him to know what you can handle and to protect you from it.

I have a minster friend that reported an encounter where he was ministering to a woman that came to him for help because she was brokenhearted and tormented by an incident in which she had been sexually assaulted by a family member. He prayed for healing for those painful emotions and afterward, she only felt some better. He decided to pray and ask God to wipe away the memory of the incident completely as well as the all of the pain. Her countenance was totally transformed. He asked her how she was feeling and said she was fine. She seemed confused as to why he was asking. He then asked her if she had ever been sexually assaulted and she responded with a very emphatic, "No!" She didn't understand why he had asked her such a thing. God can wipe away the image or memory of a specifically painful encounter, but He can also heal all of it to the point that the emotion of it will be void of pain and suffering. Please don't let the fear of facing surfaced memories hinder you from recovering your life back. Trust God to help you and know that He won't ever hurt you.

The type of memory loss people that dissociate oftentimes contend with is known as Dissociative Amnesia. There are a number of therapies and medications that can be used to treat this condition. For most people, with time, their memory will eventually return.

This book isn't about doing it the world's way, but it's about restoring lives and minds supernaturally. Let's look at some scripture to examine what God has to say about these matters. In this first passage, we see that God has given us a sound mind. Anything short of that is not of Him.

2 Timothy 1:7 For God has not given us a spirit of fear, but of power and of love and of a sound mind.

As a matter of fact, He promises us perfect peace if we keep our mind fixed on Him.

Isaiah 26:3 You will keep *him* in perfect peace, *Whose* mind *is* stayed *on You*, Because he trusts in You.

The word says the we have the mind of Christ. I imagine that would be a perfect mind. Wouldn't you agree?

1 Corinthians 2:16 For who hath known the mind of the Lord, that he may instruct him? But we have the mind of Christ.

So what if you do have a problem and can't remember something? I'm glad you asked! You have a Helper that is happy to assist you with that.

John 14:26 But the Helper, the Holy Spirit, whom the Father will send in My name, He will teach you all things, and bring to your remembrance all things that I said to you.

There are things you can do to keep yourself focused and to improve the state of your mind. The Word says we can even renew our mind.

Romans 12:2 And do not be conformed to this world, but be transformed by the renewing of your mind, that you may prove what *is* that good and acceptable and perfect will of God.

The Bible even shows us where to focus our thoughts.

Colossians 3: 1-2 If then you were raised with Christ, seek those things which are above, where Christ is, sitting at the right hand of God. Set your mind on things above, not on things on the earth.

Philippians 4:7-8 and the peace of God, which surpasses all understanding, will guard your hearts and minds through Christ Jesus. Finally, brethren, whatever things are true, whatever things *are* noble, whatever things *are* just, whatever things *are* pure, whatever things *are* lovely, whatever things *are* of good report, if *there is* any virtue and if *there is* anything praiseworthy—meditate on these things.

As you can see, whether or not it is your current experience, God has made provision for you. He has given you freedom of fear, a sound mind, perfect peace, the mind of Christ and a live in Comforter that will teach you all things and also helps you to remember them. He provides a way to renew your mind and He even tells you what to think about and where to focus your thoughts. The Creator that knew you before the foundations of the world and loves you more than you can fathom, wants you whole; spirit, soul and body. Healing awaits. Pray this prayer out loud and expect to get your memory back!

Father, I come before You without fear because I know You are with me. Your Word says I have a sound mind and the mind of Christ and that Holy Spirit will teach me all things and bring things that are needful to my remembrance. I don't know all of the memories that have been hidden from me, but You do. Whatever pain might be there, I ask that you heal those emotions and I trust that You will. I believe that Your Light can cause all of the darkness to flee, even in my darkest of days. Help me to remember again. I want my life back. Help me to remember my daily tasks and to function well in all I do. I ask in particular, to remember any time that someone showed me love, cared for me or tried to reach out to me and help. I want to remember each time You tried to reach out to me and every time

You were with me. Lord, I want to remember every beautiful day, every smile and laughter, every lovely song, every dance, raindrop and snowfall. Unlock every joy from my mind and help me to feel each one. If there weren't many, I'm still grateful for my life and for having You in it now. Thank you for freeing me from the prison of my mind and for restoring my memory. I will not forget Your goodness or Your benefits. I choose to walk in love, joy and gratitude each and every day and for the rest of my life. In Jesus name, Amen.

RESTORING DECLARATIONS

As you've gone through this book, you have spent some time getting rid of some things like unforgiveness, pain, fear, devices, soulish ties and even demons. God will not take something away from you without giving you something better. Now it's time for the better! It's time to replenish your soul with good things.

So how do you do that? As mentioned earlier in this book, just as God spoke this world into existence and created us in His image, we too, speak our own world into existence every day. Our words can change our circumstances now and start framing our future.

Proverbs 18:21 Death and life are in the power of the tongue: And those that love it will eat its fruit.

James 3:2-5 ...If anyone does not stumble in word, he *is* a perfect man, able also to bridle the whole body. Indeed, we put bits in horses' mouths that they may obey us, and we turn their whole body. Look also at ships: although they are so large

and are driven by fierce winds, they are turned by a very small rudder wherever the pilot desires. Even so the tongue is a little member and boasts great things.

Your words are very powerful and can change the course of your life. Faith makes all the difference. Faith manifests from your heart and spills out of your mouth. You say what you believe and if you speak things often enough, you will begin to believe what you say, good or bad. You broadcast your future with your own words. What are you saying? Are you blessing or cursing yourself? Is your speech filled with fear and dread? Are you talking about getting sick, being broke, losing things and how bad things are, or are you talking about your dreams, your plans, your health and how blessed you are? Your future is in your mouth and in your heart. Whatever you say and believe, you will have. If you aren't liking what you have, start saying what you want!

Luke 6:45 A good man out of the good treasure of his heart brings forth good; and an evil man out of the evil treasure of his heart brings forth evil. For out of the abundance of the heart his mouth speaks.

The best way to get heaven to back you and to start seeing results is to find out what God has said about you and agree with Him. The Bible isn't just a book, it is a living document, God's love letter to you! His Word is so powerful it is exalted above the name of Jesus and the name of Jesus is pretty powerful as it is above every other name!

Psalm 138:2 I will worship toward Your holy temple, and praise Your name for Your lovingkindness and Your truth: for You have

magnified Your word above all Your name.

Philippians 2:9-11 Therefore God also has highly exalted Him and given Him the name which is above every name, that at the name of Jesus every knee should bow, of those in heaven, and of those on earth, and of those under the earth, and *that* every tongue should confess that Jesus Christ Lord, to the glory of God the Father.

The Bible also says that God's Word will accomplish what He sent it to do.

Isaiah 55:11 So shall My word be that goes forth from My mouth; It shall not return to Me void, But it shall accomplish what I please, And it shall prosper *in the thing* for which I sent it.

The most efficient way to turn things around is to make bold declarations over yourself that agree with what God says about you and speak His promises over your circumstances. This isn't spoken just once and abandoned, but continually meditated on until you see your life transform. Make these declarations as often as it crosses your mind. Find promises in the Word you want to see come to pass. Write them down, keep them before your eyes, speak them out confidently and believe those words are life and will transform any situation in which you apply them. You may want to record your voice making these declarations and even listen to them as you sleep. Nourish your spirit with His Word. The list below is a starting point and were chosen to restore your soul. Say them out loud slowly and deliberately as you ponder each one...

I am loved.

For God so loved me that He gave His only begotten Son, and because I believe in Him, I should not perish but have everlasting life. (John 3:16)

God demonstrates His own love toward me, in that while I was still a sinner, Christ died for me. (Romans 5:8)

If God is for me, who can be against me? (Romans 8:31)

I am more than a conqueror through Him who loved me. For I am persuaded that neither death nor life, nor angels nor principalities nor powers, nor things present nor things to come, nor height nor depth, nor any other created thing, shall be able to separate me from the love of God which is in Christ Jesus my Lord. (Romans 8:37-39)

I can give Him all of my problems and fears because He cares for me. (1 Peter 5:7)

I am safe.

God *is my* refuge and strength, A very present help when I'm in trouble (Psalm 46:1)

I can lie down and sleep in peace, because He keeps me safe. (Psalm 4:8)

He will satisfy and replenish my weary and sorrowful soul. (Jeremiah 31:25)

You are my hiding place and You protect me from trouble and surround me with songs of deliverance. (Psalm 32:7)

I am not afraid.

Though I walk through the valley of the shadow of death, I will fear no evil; For You *are* with me; Your rod and Your staff, they comfort me. (Psalm 23:4)

In the multitude of my anxieties within me, Your comforts delight my soul. (Psalm 94:19)

I will be strong and of good courage, I will not fear or be afraid of them; for the Lord my God, He *is* the One who goes with me. He will not leave me nor forsake me. (Deuteronomy 31:6)

God takes my right hand and says, "Do not fear." He will help me. (Isaiah 41:13)

There is no fear in love; but perfect love casts out fear, because fear involves torment. I do not fear and have been made perfect in love. (1 John 4:18)

I have a sound mind.

God hasn't given me a spirit of fear, but one of power, love and a sound mind. (2 Timothy 1:7)

...I have the mind of Christ. (1 Corinthians 2:16)

Holy Spirit helps and teaches me all things and helps me to remember the words of Jesus. (John 14:26)

I am a new creation in Christ. Old things have passed away and all things are new. (2 Corinthians 5:17)

I am happy.

I delight in the Lord and He gives me the desires of my heart. (Psalm 37:4)

I will ask in His name and I will receive so my joy will be complete. (John 16:24)

I am at peace.

the peace of God, which surpasses all understanding, will guard my heart and mind through Christ Jesus. (Philippians 4:7)

The Lord strengthens me and blesses me with peace. (Psalm 29:11)

I will turn from evil and do good. I will seek peace and pursue it. (Psalm 34:14)

I come to Him when I'm weary or burdened and He gives me rest. (Matthew 11:28)

I am healed.

He forgives all my sins and heals all my diseases. (Psalm 103:3)

He heals my broken heart and binds up my wounds. (Psalm 147:3)

He, Himself bore my sins in His own body on the tree, that I, having died to sins, might live for righteousness—by whose stripes I was healed. (1 Peter 2:24)

...He is my God that heals me. (Exodus 15:26)

I am whole and complete.

I am complete in Him who is head of all principality and power. (Colossians 2:10)

I only believe and I am made whole. (Luke 8:50)

My faith makes me whole. (Luke 17:19)

I have a purpose.

I make plans, but the Lord directs my steps. (Proverbs 16:9)

He has saved me and called *me* with a holy calling, not according to my works, but according to His own purpose and grace which was given to me in Christ Jesus before time began. (2 Timothy 1:9)

He chose me in Him before the foundation of the world, that I should be holy and without blame before Him in love. (Ephesians 1:4)

I know that all things work together for good to those who love God, to those who are the called according to His purpose. That includes me. (Romans 8:28)

God has good plans for me to give me a future and hope. (Jeremiah 29:11)

I will never quit or give up.

I will not tire in doing good and I will reap a harvest if I don't give up. (Galatians 6:9)

Because I remain in Him and His words remain in me, I can ask what I want and it will be done for me. (John 15:7)

By my patience, I possess my soul. (Luke 21:19)

I put on the full armor of God so I can stand against the devil's schemes. (Ephesians 6:11)

I am a giver.

I give generously and willingly and the Lord blesses all of my work. (Deuteronomy 15:10)

I give, and it will be given to me: good measure, pressed down, shaken together, and running over will be put into my bosom. For with the same measure that I use, it will be measured back to me. (Luke 6:38)

I sow bountifully and will also reap bountifully. I *give* as I purpose in my heart, not grudgingly or of necessity; for God loves a cheerful giver. And God *is* able to make all grace abound toward me, that I, always having all sufficiency in all *things,* may have an abundance for every good work.
(2 Corinthians 9:6-8)

I trust God.

When I am afraid, God, I put my trust in You. (Psalm 56:3)

I trust in the Lord with all my heart and lean not on my own understanding. In all my ways I acknowledge Him and He directs my path. (Proverbs 3:5-6)

I am blessed because I trust in Him. (Psalm 84:12)

I have perfect peace and my mind is steady because I trust in Him. (Isaiah 26:3)

As for God, His way *is* perfect; The word of the Lord *is* proven; He *is* a shield to me because I trust in Him. (2 Samuel 22:31)

MIND CONTROL PROGRAMMING

A traumatic experience such as repeated abuse as a child, sex trafficking, acts of war, viewing something particularly horrific like a murder or suicide and any number of things can cause dissociation. When one has been a victim of a cult or has experienced SRA, there can be added complications and torment due to demonization. When it comes to mind control programming, the plot thickens even more because of the complexity of the process and the way the mind is purposefully manipulated, oftentimes from a very early age. Most dissociation is a by-product of trauma. In the case of mind control, particularly with Monarch programming, the goal is to cause the subject to dissociate. No, that wasn't a typo. The GOAL is to cause the person to dissociate so that they may be controlled.

All cases are different, but the most sinister programming usually starts when a baby is just a few months old. The training may start when the very impressionable mind of a young child has primary needs like love, food, milk and toys withheld for long periods at a time. They are often left alone all day and when food or some other necessity is brought to them, they are physically punished for grabbing at it. They are often taught to trust only one person that will eventually betray them with "betrayal programming". Oftentimes they are introduced to another child and preferably a twin, that they will bond with and get close to, share secrets with and will ultimately be taught to betray them as well during "twinning programming". Some children become expendable and are sometimes tortured or murdered in front of other children as a fear tactic. The survivors will often be told they were to blame for the killing because they didn't obey. As they grow, the methods become more varied with a number of torture techniques applied to obtain the needed result. Electroshock, drugging, skinning, sexual assault, torture using bright lights, spinning, forced impregnation and abortion, incest, chemical baths, beatings and "marriage" to satan are just a few of the techniques used.

These children may grow up be be sex slaves with girls as young as six years old being photographed in provocative poses wearing lingerie and high heels with full makeup and adult hairstyles. These girls have usually been subjected to "kitten programming". Other forms of programming might produce sleeper assassins, diplomats, couriers and mules. Research will help you learn more than you'd probably ever care to know about the dark secrets of mind control. The origins are frightening. The CIA would have you believe that their "experiments" are no longer being done, but sadly, these activities are shockingly real and widespread.

Over the course of their childhood and adolescence, victims are tortured and subjected to many layers of mind manipulation. This results in something that would resemble a very complex video gaming system with scenery of numerous levels, traps, set-ups, punishments, goals, codes, cues, images, triggers and a myriad of complexity to control the subject to do the bidding of the handler and group they represent. It may be the Illuminati, an agency, a military, a government or the entertainment industry. I use the word, subject, because that is how they are treated, however they are people with minds, hearts and emotions that have become victims of horrid circumstances. Although they are understandably cautious, distrusting, fearful, hurt and emotionally damaged with a very complex past, God loves them and wants to see them set free and to live the life He purposed for them. We are to love them, and carry them till they can walk on their own.

What might seem impossible is possible with God. This book in its entirety, will help the victims of mind control. There needs to be both healing and deliverance ministered with patience and love. Some sections may need to be visited more than once. The restoring declarations should be done often to get the Word of God operating in your heart. Meditating in the scriptures will help renew your mind and the prayers within these pages can be said as often as needed. In the back section of this book are specific prayers for various forms of trauma. The specific prayers for mind control found in the next section will be very helpful. Persevere and trust in God. Have faith and patience. Be good to yourself, accept God's love and the love of others. Only believe. The best is yet to come. Remember, there is life after brokenness.

MORE SPECIFIC PRAYERS FOR YOUR CIRCUMSTANCES

I've done it. More times than not, I do it. I jump to the part of a "how to" or "self help" book that I think will sum up my need's answer in the quickest amount of time. Then, if I find I need to go back and find something in the material, I'll jump to the Table of Contents to find the next page to search. After I've found what I needed, the book is then put away to hold onto for a reference if ever I should need it again.

If you've started here, you are missing the whole point of this guide. There are no quick answers for those that dissociate, aside from a miraculous deliverance from God. Is that possible? Absolutely! All things are possible to him that believes, however, you didn't get here in one day. This can be quite complex and in God's grace, trying to rush through a forest of pain to get to the other side may not be in your best interest. Just as a baby chick pecks away from the inside of its shell until it becomes strong enough to break though, you may need to be strengthened, healed and made whole before you'll see your breakthrough. All the while, God wants you to grow and heal as He watches over your every step. Embrace the process. This book is designed to deal with every aspect of recovery, one layer at a time. These prayers have been added as a quick overview and to distinguish different things to address, depending on the origin or type of trauma.

Please read through the book at least once and pray through the prayers as you go, because they will not all be found in this section. Say these prayers boldly and confidently that what you say will come to pass in the Mighty Name of Jesus!

TRAUMA

I bind and break every trigger, every trigger word and every image RIGHT NOW! Any manipulation or witchcraft, I bind and break and render it null and void! It has no more power over you. I bind any demonic activity in and around you NOW! I bind any effects from alcohol or drugs and command them to be broken now! I bind any programming that you've been subjected to now! I declare your mind is free from binding influences and you are now able to think clearly for yourself.

If you are not already, become born again. Receive the Lord into your heart. Ask for forgiveness of all your sins and, in your own way, ask God to change your life; to change your heart and to live in you and accept you as His child.

I apply the blood of Jesus over me and ask You, Father, for Your help in getting through this process to set me free.

Prayers to forgive your perpetrator, any accomplice, anyone that helped them or anyone that turned their head and didn't help you; prayers to forgive yourself and God as needed. Forgive each person individually and release them. Release those thoughts that hinder and cripple you, even if you feel justified to hold resentment. (There is much more detailed instruction in the section on forgiveness)

(See the section in the text to find the following prayers)
Prayers concerning Fear
Prayers dealing with Self Worth
Prayers to quiet Voices in your Mind (May Not Apply)

Deliverance and Addressing Demonic Activity
Dealing with Devices (May Not Apply)
Breaking Harmful Soul Ties
Prayers Pertaining to Painful Memories and/or Memory Loss
Restoring Declarations

Father, in the name of Jesus, I ask You to erase the most painful images in my mind and to heal my emotions from the trauma I have endured. I command all fear and the fear of reoccurrence, all grief, anxiety, depression, anger, bitterness and isolation to GO NOW! I command any addictions, nightmares, thoughts of suicide and anything I do to sabotage myself or my future to cease and desist NOW in Jesus name!

Lord, I thank You for healing me, spirit, soul and body and making me whole. I thank You for Your provision and protection, for Your guidance and direction, but mostly for Your love. I love You and thank You for all You are and do. Amen.

POST TRAUMATIC STRESS DISORDER

I bind and break every trigger, every trigger word, every image, every cue and hypnotic suggestion RIGHT NOW! I bind the power of mind control and I command it to be broken and of no effect NOW! Any manipulation or witchcraft, I bind and break and render it null and void! It has no more power over you. Any devices that have been implanted in you to control you, whether they be chips, pins, webs or ports, I break their power over you. I bind any demonic activity in and around you NOW! I bind any effects from alcohol or drugs and command them to be broken now! I bind any programming that you've been subjected to now! I declare your mind is free from binding influences and you are now able to think clearly for yourself.

If you are not already, become born again. Receive the Lord into your heart. Ask for forgiveness of all your sins and, in your own way, ask God to change your life; to change your heart and to live in you and accept you as His child.

I apply the blood of Jesus over me and ask You, Father, for Your help in getting through this process to set me free.

Prayers to forgive your perpetrator, any accomplice, anyone that helped them or anyone that turned their head and didn't help you; prayers to forgive yourself and God as needed. Forgive each person individually and release them. Release those thoughts that hinder and cripple you, even if you feel justified to hold resentment. (There is much more detailed instruction in the section on forgiveness)

(See the section in the text to find the following prayers)
Prayers concerning Fear
Prayers dealing with Self Worth
Prayers to quiet Voices in your Mind (May Not Apply)
Deliverance and Addressing Demonic Activity
Dealing with Devices (May Not Apply)
Breaking Harmful Soul Ties
Prayers Pertaining to Painful Memories and/or Memory Loss
Restoring Declarations

Father, in the name of Jesus, I ask You to erase the most painful images in my mind and to heal my emotions from the trauma I have endured. I command all fear and the fear of reoccurrence, all grief, anxiety, depression, anger, bitterness and isolation to GO NOW! I command shock and loud noises to no longer trouble me. I command any addictions, nightmares, thoughts of suicide and anything I do to sabotage myself or my future to cease and desist NOW in Jesus name!

Lord, I thank You for healing me, spirit, soul and body and making me whole. I thank You for Your provision and protection, for Your guidance and direction, but mostly for Your love. I love You and thank You for all You are and do. Amen

SATANIC RITUAL ABUSE

I bind and break every trigger, every trigger word, every image, every cue and hypnotic suggestion RIGHT NOW! I bind the power of mind control and I command it to be broken and of no effect NOW! Any manipulation or witchcraft, I bind and break and render it null and void! It has no more power over you. Any devices that have been implanted in you to control you, whether they be chips, pins, webs or ports, I break their power over you. I bind any demonic activity in and around you NOW! I bind any effects from alcohol or drugs and command them to be broken now! I bind any programming that you've been subjected to now! I declare your mind is free from binding influences and you are now able to think clearly for yourself.

If you are not already, become born again. Receive the Lord into your heart. Ask for forgiveness of all your sins and, in your own way, ask God to change your life; to change your heart and to live in you and accept you as His child.

I apply the blood of Jesus over me and ask You, Father, for Your help in getting through this process to set me free.

Prayers to forgive your perpetrator, any accomplice, anyone that helped them or anyone that turned their head and didn't help you; prayers to forgive yourself and God as needed. Forgive each person individually and release them. Release those thoughts that hinder and cripple you, even if you feel justified to hold resentment. (There is much more detailed instruction in the section on forgiveness)

(See the section in the text to find the following prayers)
Prayers concerning Fear
Prayers dealing with Self Worth
Prayers to quiet Voices in your Mind (May Not Apply)
Deliverance and Addressing Demonic Activity
Dealing with Devices (May Not Apply)
Breaking Harmful Soul Ties
Prayers Pertaining to Painful Memories and/or Memory Loss
Restoring Declarations

Father, in the name of Jesus, I ask You to erase the most painful images in my mind and to heal my emotions from the trauma I have endured. I command all fear and the fear of reoccurrence, all grief, anxiety, depression, anger, bitterness and isolation to GO NOW! I command any addictions, nightmares, thoughts of suicide and anything I do to sabotage myself or my future to cease and desist NOW in Jesus name!

I break the power of all forms of witchcraft, the Illuminati and Freemasonry over my life now as though it were naught. I undo anything a satanic priest, witch or warlock or handler has done against me and NO weapon formed against me will prosper. I break every ungodly covenant, satanic ritual, any spell, all hexes, incantations, blood oaths, curses and the power of anything that tries to pull me to return now, in Jesus name!

I command any spirits that cause mutilation, self harm, and cutting to leave me NOW and never return. All tormenting, mind binding and lying

spirits, SHUT UP and get out NOW! Trauma and rejection GO and never return in Jesus name!

Lord, I thank You for healing me, spirit, soul and body and making me whole. I thank You for Your provision and protection, for Your guidance and direction, but mostly for Your love. I love You and thank You for all You are and do. Amen.

MIND CONTROL PROGRAMMING

I bind and break every trigger, every trigger word, every image, every cue and hypnotic suggestion RIGHT NOW! I bind the power of mind control and I command it to be broken and of no effect NOW! Any manipulation or witchcraft, I bind and break and render it null and void! It has no more power over you. Any devices that have been implanted in you to control you, whether they be chips, pins, webs or ports, I break their power over you. I bind any demonic activity in and around you NOW! I bind any effects from alcohol or drugs and command them to be broken now! I bind any programming that you've been subjected to now! I declare your mind is free from binding influences and you are now able to think clearly for yourself.

If you are not already, become born again. Receive the Lord into your heart. Ask for forgiveness of all your sins and, in your own way, ask God to change your life; to change your heart and to live in you and accept you as His child.

I apply the blood of Jesus over me and ask You, Father, for Your help in getting through this process to set me free.

Prayers to forgive your perpetrator, any accomplice, anyone that helped them or anyone that turned their head and didn't help you; prayers to forgive yourself and God as needed. Forgive each person individually and release them. Release those thoughts that hinder and cripple you, even if you feel justified to hold resentment. (There is much more detailed instruction in the section on forgiveness)

(See the section in the text to find the following prayers)
Prayers concerning Fear
Prayers dealing with Self Worth
Prayers to quiet Voices in your Mind (May Not Apply)
Deliverance and Addressing Demonic Activity
Dealing with Devices (May Not Apply)
Breaking Harmful Soul Ties
Prayers Pertaining to Painful Memories and/or Memory Loss
Restoring Declarations

Father, in the name of Jesus, I ask You to erase the most painful images in my mind and to heal my emotions from the trauma I have endured. I command all fear and the fear of reoccurrence, all grief, anxiety, depression, anger, bitterness and isolation to GO NOW! I command any addictions, nightmares, thoughts of suicide and anything I do to sabotage myself or my future to cease and desist NOW in Jesus name!

In the name of Jesus, I dissolve all amnesic barriers between personalities and command all memory of torture be removed. I remove all gatekeepers and blockers and break the seal of every stairwell. I remove every number, alphabet, and rhyme code, every booby trap and all suicidal programming. I remove all erasure codes, block codes, stop codes and brain switch commands and I dissolve any grids or clone grids and command no more clones to be generated ever again. I undo every hypnotic and visual cue, visual landscape and projected image such as castle, carousel, Kabul, umbrella, puppet and cave. I command every level,

secret, hazard or danger to be safely restored to God's design without any harm NOW in Jesus name!

I command any self destruct programming to cease and any suicide or self mutilation programs to be broken. All tornado or whirlwind programs be dissolved and Systems including Spider Web, Carousel, Pool of Death, Communication, Kabbala, Puppet, Pentagram, Tornado, Castle, Galaxy, Flower, Scrabble, and Umbrella systems be dissolved NOW! All things associated with "military" mind control programming such as: Double Helix, Solometric, Cave and Well, and the Mensa systems be broken and as of naught NOW in Jesus name! I break every connector, silk strand and clone strand and command no new webs be spun in Jesus name. I remove the viper, its eggs and all poison. I delete any criss-cross programming. I break all numeric, sequencing, bar codes and union force codes and command its DNA connection to be broken and command the blood to be cleaned by the blood of Jesus. I command the mirror and shadow system to be broken and command the false prophet, hoofed one and dragon spirits to leave NOW in Jesus name! I command all mathematical sequencing deleted in Jesus name!

I break the power of any type of twinning programming and shatter any betrayal programming NOW in Jesus name! I break every form or created internal structure and tear down any temple erected to any false god or entity including Moloch, Ra, the sun god and Horus NOW! I tear down any pyramid, geometric figure, training grid, columns, computers, robots, crystals, mirrors, carousels, deck of cards, black boxes, mines, internal training rooms, walls and seals NOW in the name of Jesus! I repent from any blood and satanic sacrifice that was made on my behalf for any reason and ask every sacrificial alter to be torn down. I denounce the blood sacrifice(s) and ask they no longer have a voice against me.

I break the power of all forms of witchcraft, the Illuminati and Freemasonry over my life now as though it were naught. I undo anything a satanic priest, witch or warlock or handler has done against me and NO weapon formed against me will prosper. I command all forms of mind control to be broken and all access to me from the enemy be shut off permanently. I break any ungodly tie any government or industry has to me and I thwart any blackmail and break any threat to me, my loved ones or my livelihood in Jesus name. Any attempt to control me with drugs or poison will fail. I come against any slander or tongue that rises up against me and command it to cease. No plan against me will come to fruition. I break every ungodly covenant, satanic ritual, any spell, all hexes, incantations, blood oaths, curses and the power of anything that tries to pull me to return now, in Jesus name!

I command any spirits that cause mutilation, self harm, and cutting to leave me NOW and never return. All tormenting, mind binding and lying spirits, SHUT UP and get out NOW! Trauma and rejection GO and never return in Jesus name!

Lord, I thank You for healing me, spirit, soul and body and making me whole. I thank You for Your provision and protection, for Your guidance and direction, but mostly for Your love. I love You and thank You for all You are and do. Amen.

Made in the USA
Columbia, SC
23 January 2019